SharePoint Workflows

from Scratch

Peter Kalmström

SHAREPOINT WORKFLOWS FROM SCRATCH

Welcome to *SharePoint Workflows from Scratch*! This book gives the basic knowledge needed to automate SharePoint business processes with workflows, whether you manage a SharePoint on-premises farm or use SharePoint Online in an Office 365 tenancy.

SharePoint Workflows from Scratch is intended for SharePoint administrators, content creators and other power users who already know their way around SharePoint. (If you are new to SharePoint, you will find my book *SharePoint Online from Scratch* more useful.)

SharePoint workflows are suitable for all kinds of SharePoint lists and libraries where you want to automate time consuming or repetitive processes. Workflows are often used for notification sending, but they can also calculate time, archive list items and perform many other tasks that would have been tedious – or not performed at all – if they were not automated.

In my work as a SharePoint consultant, I have come to understand what automation areas are the most important to SharePoint power users, and the book focuses on those areas.

The questions I get are most often concrete – "How do I …?, or "Can SharePoint …?" – and I hope this book will give the answers to the most common of them. Therefore, *SharePoint Workflows from Scratch* has many images and step by step instructions, and to be even clearer, I often refer to my online video demonstrations.

SharePoint Workflows from Scratch begins with a few chapters of basic information. After that, I give concrete examples of how workflows can be used to automate common business processes. When selecting these example workflows, I have first considered which examples are most useful for business process automation.

Only in the second place, I have considered which examples show new features. I have however introduced something new in each example workflow and tried to arrange them in an order that creates a good progression.

I recommend that you actually create these example workflows yourself and not just read about them. That way you will learn to manage SharePoint workflows, and you will discover a lot more about them than I have included in the book.

I hope that when you have finished this book, you should have enough knowledge to continue exploring the workflow possibilities on your own

Good luck with your studies!

Peter Kalmström

TABLE OF CONTENTS

1   WHY AUTOMATE?

Before we start looking into the workflows, I will point out why you should automate business processes in the first place. As you are reading this book, you probably already know why, but maybe you will still find it useful to have my opinion on the benefits of SharePoint automation compared to manual processes.

You might also find these points relevant in discussions with others. "Why don't we just do this manually?" is still a common question.

1.1   ACCURACY

Most organizations have processes that need to be performed in a specific way and order, and the best way to make sure that they are really performed this way, is to automate them. When processes are performed manually, you can never be sure that everything is done 100% correctly.

People make mistakes. Even if you check and double-check your work there will be errors, and these are often difficult to find. People also get bored and are prone to do variations, which might lead to further mistakes.

A workflow, on the other hand, always works in the same way. Once you have tested the workflow and made sure that it works as it should, you can rely on its accuracy. The workflow follows the same process. in the same way, every time. It does not make mistakes or variations now and then, like we humans do.

Another factor is that human errors often are random, which makes them hard to find and correct. If a workflow does something wrong, it at least does it consistently wrong – making the same mistake in every run.

1.2   TRACKING

With a workflow, it is easy to track processes. Workflows can log and document what has been done, something that is often requested by the management and sometimes even by law. Such tasks are often tedious and boring to perform manually and tend to be performed insufficiently or not at all.

When you let workflows keep track of what happens, you will also have documentation. A workflow can for example add items in a SharePoint list or comments in a list column describing what has been done and why.

1.3 SPEED

It takes time to build a workflow, but the workflow creation time will be well spent if you have a process that must be performed repeatedly. Once the workflow is tested and works well, no more time has to be spent on the process, but to do it manually takes time over and over again.

Furthermore, the workflow in itself is quicker than a human. Even if workflows normally have a short delay, they perform most processes much quicker than humans can do.

Demo:

https://www.kalmstrom.com/Tips/SharePoint-Workflows/Why-Automate.htm

1.4 FLOW OR WORKFLOW?

In 2016, Microsoft introduced a new service for workflow creation: Flow. Workflows created with Flow are sometimes called "workflows" and sometimes "flows", but in this book, I will reserve the term "workflow" for the built-in SharePoint automation templates and for custom automation processes created in *SharePoint Designer*.

Flows can be used with many different apps and services, as long as they are cloud-based. This is not true for workflows. Almost all workflow actions are restricted to content within one single SharePoint site.

As Microsoft Flow is a cloud-based service, it is mostly used with SharePoint Online and not with SharePoint on-premises. I have described how to use Microsoft Flow in my book *SharePoint Flows from Scratch.*

However, even if your organization uses SharePoint Online, you should learn to manage both flows and workflows. That way, you can choose the best option for every situation and process. You also need to learn workflows for another reason: your organization probably already has a lot of workflows that make processes quicker and more efficient.

Flow is a more modern solution than the traditional workflows, but the workflows are still useful inside SharePoint and there the flows cannot do everything that is possible with a workflow. Sometimes, when both options are possible, you might still want to use a workflow.

One of the workflow benefits is that workflows don't use the caption of the lists and columns, but the internal name, a GUID. This means that the workflow will keep running even if you change the name of a list or column. If you change a list or column name that is used in a flow, on the other hand, you must change in the flow also. Otherwise it will stop working.

So, my recommendation to SharePoint power users is to learn both. With that knowledge, you will have all the possibilities, and you can judge which option to use in each case. And even if you have SharePoint Online and prefer to use Flow when possible, you can still manage the organization's existing workflows.

Demo:

https://www.kalmstrom.com/Tips/SharePoint-Workflows/SharePoint-No-Code-Automation.htm

2 WORKFLOW BASICS

In the last ten years, workflows have been the traditional way of automating business processes in all kinds of SharePoint editions, online and on-premises. Microsoft has given us a few built-in workflows, but other SharePoint workflows are created in a free designer tool for SharePoint, *SharePoint Designer*.

The principle of all automation is that you select conditions to be met and actions to be taken when these conditions are met. A predefined trigger decides when the workflow should start running.

The sequence is always that a workflow is started by a trigger and then it starts running. During the workflow run it will encounter conditions and actions, and these will be executed in the order they are written, from top to bottom.

2.1 TRIGGERS

The trigger decides in general when the workflow should be run. A trigger can be manual or automatic. When a workflow is created with an automatic trigger, there is often a possibility to start it manually also, if needed.

You will learn more about triggers in chapter 7 of this book.

2.2 CONDITIONS

In a sense, workflows are written in a programming language, and like all programming languages the workflows have conditions that control under which circumstances things happen during the workflow run.

For example, a condition can be that some actions are only to be performed when a task in a task list has the column Priority set to 'High'. To achieve this, the workflow should include a condition that checks the value of the Priority column. The actions to be performed in this case are said to be "enclosed within the condition". That is visually indicated by the actions being slightly indented.

There is no such thing as a "conditional trigger". If the workflow is intended to perform actions only in some cases, you need to enclose those actions inside a condition. The workflow will run in every case, but it will only perform actions if the condition evaluates to true.

In other programming languages, a condition is usually referred to as an "if statement". This is how it would look in the programming language PowerShell, for example:

```
If($Priority -eq "High"){

        Send-Email -To "peter@kalmstrom.com -Subject "New task"

}
```

Notice that, like in a workflow, the Send-Email action will only be executed if $Priority is indeed equal to "High" and that the action is written indented to show that it is enclosed.

When a workflow has been started by a trigger, the running means that it evaluates conditions and executes actions.

2.3 ACTIONS

The workflow actions decide what parameters the workflow should affect and what should be done with them.

A common action is 'Send an Email'. When that action is used, the receiver, subject and body text of the message is defined in the action.

There are a lot of actions to select from, and they can be combined with conditions so that a series of actions are performed under certain conditions. There are also actions that start workflows.

You will learn a lot more about different conditions and actions in 8.2, Actions and Conditions, and in the example workflows I provide later in this book.

2.4 SEE WORKFLOW STATUS

Once the workflow has started running, a status column with the same name as the workflow will be created in the SharePoint list that the workflow is connected to.

When the workflow is running, you can see the workflow status at the item that triggered the workflow – provided that the box for manual start has been kept checked (which is default) in the "Workflow Settings" page in *SharePoint Designer*.

☑ Automatically update the workflow status to the current stage name

It is often suitable to hide the status column from the default view when the workflow is tested and should go in production.

2.4.1 The "Workflow Status" Page

When the status column is displayed in a list, click on the text in the column to open the "Workflow Status" page.

If the status column is hidden in the list, you can reach the "Workflow Status" page via the list item ellipsis >More >Workflow (modern interface) or Advanced >Workflows (classic). Click on a workflow under 'Running Workflows' to see its status page.

This page is created automatically when the first workflow on a site is run for the first time. Here you can see which steps or stages a running workflow goes through. That way, you can follow the process in detail.

In the "Workflow Status" page you can also terminate the workflow and see workflow history. Workflow history is maintained for 60 days after completion.

The "Workflow Tasks" list is embedded in the page. This list is also created automatically by the first workflow. I will come back to this list in the example workflow in chapter 27, New Employee Tasks.

3   BUILT-IN WORKFLOWS

SharePoint has a few built-in workflow templates, and even if this book focuses on how you build your own workflows, I will start with an introduction to what you already have available in SharePoint.

The built-in workflow templates have some modification options, but you cannot at all customize them in the same way as when you create workflows from scratch in *SharePoint Designer*, which we will do in the major part of this book.

All the built-in workflows create tasks. These tasks can be reached in the "Workflow Tasks" list, which is created automatically by each site's first workflow. This list is also used for custom workflows, and by default, it is displayed in the Quick Launch after creation. *Refer to* 27.1.3, The "Workflow Tasks" List, for more info.

3.1   ADD A WORKFLOW

To add a workflow to a list or library, open the List/Library settings >Workflow settings and add a workflow.

When you have clicked on 'Add a workflow', you can select a workflow template, give it a name and decide how the workflow should be started: manually, when an item is created and/or when an item is changed. If the list uses major and minor draft versions, the workflow can also be run at major version changes.

By default, the workflows can be manually run by all users who have edit permission on the list. You need to be a list manager to add a workflow, and as such you can also limit the manual runs to list managers.

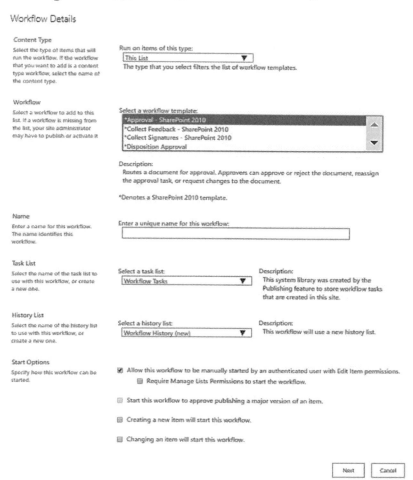

3.2 REMOVE A WORKFLOW

Under the Workflow settings, you can also remove the workflow. If you select 'No New Instances', the workflows in progress will be completed before the workflow is removed from the list.

Settings ▸ Remove Workflows ⓘ

Workflow Details

SharePoint 2013 Workflows

Select the workflows to remove from this document library. Removing a workflow association cancels its running workflows. Select No New Instances to allow running workflows to complete.

Workflow	Instances	Allow	No New Instances	Remove
There are no SharePoint 2013 Workflows associated with this list.				

SharePoint 2010 Workflows

Select the workflows to remove from this document library. Removing a workflow association cancels its running workflows. Select No New Instances to allow running workflows to complete.

Workflow	Instances	Allow	No New Instances	Remove
Approval-3	0	◉	◉	◉

OK	Cancel

3.3 THE THREE-STATE WORKFLOW

One of the built-in workflow templates in SharePoint is the Three-state workflow. It tracks the status of a list item through three phases, or states, for example Not Started, In Progress, and Finished.

The Three-state workflow creates two tasks, one when it has been initiated, and one when the first task has been completed.

This workflow can be used in any list that has a mandatory choice column with three or more values. The values in this column will serve as the phases tracked by the workflow. When you customize the workflow, you can decide which of the choice values that should be used for the three states.

When you add the Three-state workflow to a list, you must also decide what will happen when the workflow starts running and when it enters its second phase.

Workflow states:

Select a 'Choice' field, and then select a value for the initial, middle, and final states. For an Issues list, the states for an item are specified by the Status field, where:

Initial State = Active
Middle State = Resolved
Final State = Closed

As the item moves through the various stages of the workflow, the item is updated automatically.

Select a 'Choice' field:

| Phase | ▼ |

Initial state

| Not Started | ▼ |

Middle state

| In Progress | ▼ |

Final state

| Completed | ▼ |

Specify what you want to happen when a workflow is initiated:

For example, when a workflow is initiated on an issue in an Issues list, Microsoft SharePoint Foundation creates a task for the assigned user. When the user completes the task, the workflow changes from its initial state (Active) to its middle state (Resolved). You can also choose to send an e-mail message to notify the assigned user of the task.

Task Details:

Task Title:

Custom message: | Workflow initiated: |

The value for the field selected is concatenated to the custom message.

☑ Include list field: | Title ▼ |

Task Description:

Custom message: | A workflow has been initiat |

☑ Include list field: | Description ▼ |

☑ Insert link to List item

Task Due Date:

☑ Include list field: | Modified ▼ |

Task Assigned To:

◉ Include list field: | Created By ▼ |

◯ Custom: | | 👤📇

E-mail Message Details:

☑ Send e-mail message

To:

| | ☑ Include Task Assigned To

Subject:

| | ☑ Use Task Title

Process example:

1. A support request is entered as a new item in an Issue tracking list that has three phases: First level, Second level and Solved.

2. The workflow starts running and creates a task for the person that is designated for the first level.

3. The first level worker marks the task as completed.

4. The workflow updates the status of the item in the Issue Tracking list from First level to Second level.

5. The workflow creates a task for the person that is designated for the second level.

6. The second level worker completes the task.

7. The workflow updates the status of the item in the Issue Tracking list from Second level to Solved.

An e-mail about the new task can be sent automatically to the first level and/or second level people, depending on workflow settings.

3.4   2010 WORKFLOWS

There are two kinds of workflows: SharePoint 2010 workflows and SharePoint 2013 workflows. Later versions of SharePoint support both these workflow types, and I describe the differences between them in chapter 5. In the context of built-in workflow templates, it is enough that you know there are four similar templates of the type SharePoint 2010.

The 2010 workflow templates are:

- Approval: routes a document or other item to designated people for their approval or rejection. You can also use an Approval workflow to control content approval in a list or library, so that new items and/or new versions of current items must be approved before they are made visible to everyone who has access to the list or library.

- Publishing Approval: an approval workflow that is designed for SharePoint publishing sites.

- Collect Feedback: routes a document or other item to designated people for their feedback, consolidates all feedback from participants and provides a record of the review process.

- Collect Signatures: routes Microsoft Word or Excel documents or InfoPath forms to designated people for their digital signatures.

The 2010 workflow templates are not activated by default. Instead, a site administrator must activate them at Site settings >Site collection features.

When the built-in workflow templates have been activated, they can be selected in all the site collection's lists, libraries and content types. This is done under 'Workflow settings' in the settings for that list, library or content type, *see* 3.1, Add a Workflow, above.

When the basic workflow parameters have been filled out, click on 'Next' to customize the workflow further. The image below shows the Approval workflow, but the other two workflow templates are nearly the same.

Approvers	Assign To		Order
		🔍📇	One at a time (serial) ▼

☑ Add a new stage

Enter the names of the people to whom the workflow will assign tasks, and choose the order in which those tasks are assigned. Separate them with semicolons. You can also add stages to assign tasks to more people in different orders.

Expand Groups	☑ For each group entered, assign a task to every individual member and to each group that it contains.
Request	This message will be sent to the people assigned tasks.
Due Date for All Tasks	The date by which all tasks are due.
Duration Per Task	The amount of time until a task is due. Choose the units by using the Duration Units.
Duration Units	Day(s) ▼ Define the units of time used by the Duration Per Task.
CC	🔍📇 Notify these people when the workflow starts and ends without assigning tasks to them.
End on First Rejection	☐ Automatically reject the document if it is rejected by any participant.
End on Document Change	☐ Automatically reject the document if it is changed before the workflow is completed.
Enable Content Approval	☐ Update the approval status after the workflow is completed (use this workflow to control content approval).

[Save] [Cancel]

Multiple designated people can be used, and they can work with the item in serial or in parallel. The task form has fields for consolidated comments and buttons for various actions, *see* images under each workflow below.

The workflow creates a new status column in the list where it will run. This column cannot be customized and not updated by another workflow than the built-in one, and it is not visible in the list settings.

The built-in 2010 workflow templates are of course convenient to use, but they have some drawbacks:

- The list does not show the name of the person who has reacted to the document. You must go into the Workflow Status page to see that.
- You cannot specify a condition for the workflow to run, for example only for a specific file type or content type.

- Users who can start the workflow manually will also be able to change the workflow settings.

This is the general process when one of the built-in 2010 workflows runs:

1. The status column in the list gets a "pending" or "in progress" value.

2. Tasks for the designated people are added to an automatically created tasks list, by default called *Workflow Tasks*. You can see this list embedded in the 'Workflow Status' page. The tasks have links to the item that triggered the workflow.

3. E-mails with a link to the item and an 'Open this Task' button are sent to the designated people. Note that this button is only available in the e-mail ribbon in the Outlook desktop version, not in Outlook Web Access.

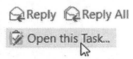

4. A "process started" e-mail with links to the item is sent to the creator of the item (and to people entered at 'cc' in the workflow settings.)

5. The designated people react to the new task, for example approves or rejects the new item, asks for changes or reassigns the task.

6. An e-mail is sent to the creator (and to cc people) with the result.

7. The status column in the list is updated.

3.4.1   Approval

The Approval workflow routes items in the list that is monitored to designated people for review and approvals. It assigns tasks and tracks their progress and sends reminders and notifications when needed. The Approval workflow is often combined with the content approval setting, *see* below.

Status	Not Started
Requested By	Kate Kalmström;
Consolidated Comments	Approval started by Kate Kalmström on 12/14/2018 1:43 PM Comment: These are the comments of the requestor and all previous participants.
Due Date	
Comments	This message will be included in your response.

Approve **Reject** **Cancel** **Request Change** **Reassign Task**

3.4.1.1   Content Approval

SharePoint lists and document libraries have an approval setting, which is disabled by default. When it is enabled, each new or changed item must be approved, so I recommend that you use separate lists and libraries for these items.

Enable content approval at List/Library settings >Versioning settings. An 'Approval Status' column will now be created automatically. This column is not visible in the settings.

Settings ▸ Versioning Settings

Content Approval

Specify whether new items or changes to existing items should remain in a draft state until they have been approved. Learn about requiring approval.

Require content approval for submitted items?

⦿ Yes ⦾ No

When the approval setting is enabled, you can also decide who will see the document or item before it has been approved. By default, only the creator and users who can approve items can see it. Only when the item has been approved, will it be shown to all users of that list or library.

Approvals can of course be handled without a workflow, but it is suitable to use content approvals with the built-in Approval workflow. If you have already enabled content approval, the workflow will make use of the 'Approval Status' column instead of creating a separate status column.

Note that the automatically created status column cannot be updated by a custom workflow. For that, you must use a custom status column. With a custom column, there is however no way to securely prevent all users from seeing the latest version of the item, even if it has not been approved.

Demos:

https://www.kalmstrom.com/Tips/SharePoint-Workflows/Approvals-without-Workflow.htm

https://www.kalmstrom.com/Tips/SharePoint-Workflows/Approvals-with-built-in-Workflow.htm

3.4.2 Publishing Approval

The Publishing Approval workflow works like the Approval workflow, but it is specially designed for SharePoint publishing sites. No new content will be published until it has been approved by every approver in the workflow.

3.4.3 Collect Feedback

Use the Collect Feedback workflow to route documents and other items stored in SharePoint products to one or more people for their feedback. It works in the same way as the Approval workflow but has different reaction options.

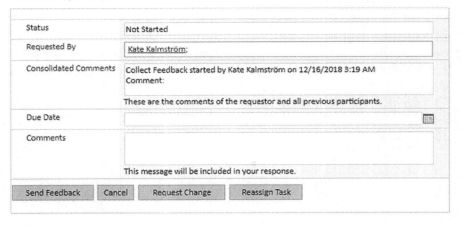

3.4.4 Collect Signatures

With a SharePoint Collect Signatures workflow, you can route documents created in Excel, Word or InfoPath to one or more people for their signatures.

Workflow Tasks: This document requires your signature

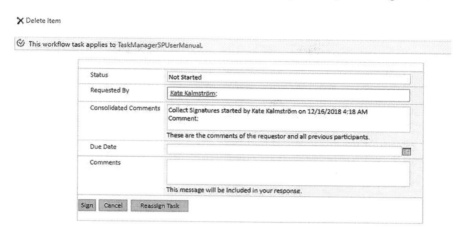

For more detailed information about the built-in workflow templates, *refer to* https://support.office.com/en-us/article/overview-of-workflows-included-with-sharepoint-d74fcceb-3a64-40fb-9904-cc33ca49da56

3.5   CHANGE ALERTS

The alerts that can be enabled in SharePoint lists are mini-workflows that send e-mail notifications when an item has been created or changed. The general alerts that are present in all lists have some possibilities to customize when the messages should be sent.

The built-in alerts have no possibility to customize the e-mail. If you, for example, want to customize the body of the e-mail that is sent out, you must let it be generated by a workflow.

3.5.1   General Alerts

All SharePoint lists have an 'Alert me' command that lets users have e-mail messages when something has been changed in a list, or when a specific item has been changed.

The site collection administrator can set alerts to be sent to other users, and each user can also set his/her own alerts.

The 'Alert Me' link can be found under the ellipsis in the modern command bar. The classic interface has buttons under the ITEMS and LIST tabs in the ribbon.

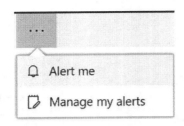

Both interfaces also have 'Alert me' links for single items under the item ellipsis.

The e-mail alerts can be somewhat customized, because you can decide at what time they should be sent and for what changes.

All alerts for one site can be managed in the same place, so the inbuilt SharePoint alerts are easy to use and a good option for change notifications. The message you get has relevant information and a link to the item.

Demo: https://kalmstrom.com/Tips/SharePoint-Online-Course/HelpDesk-Alerts.htm

3.5.2   Tasks and Issue Tracking Alerts

SharePoint lists that build on the Tasks and Issue Tracking templates have two alert possibilities that are not present in other apps:

- The Alert settings has a view selection under "Send me an alert when'.

  ⦿ Someone changes an item that appears in the following view:

  | My Issues   ▼ |

- Under 'Advanced settings' in the List settings there is a choice to send an e-mail to the person who has been assigned a task. The default value is 'No'.

E-Mail Notification

Send e-mail when ownership is assigned or when an item has been changed.

Send e-mail when ownership is assigned?

◉ Yes   ⦿ No

Demo:

https://kalmstrom.com/Tips/SharePoint-Online-Course/HelpDesk-Email-Notification.htm

4   SHAREPOINT DESIGNER

SharePoint Designer is a free desktop application that
SharePoint administrators can use for developing the
SharePoint platform.

If you want to be a SharePoint power user, you should have
SharePoint Designer installed. The 2013 version is essential
to create workflows, but you can also use *SharePoint Designer* for other
tasks.

In this chapter you will learn how to find *SharePoint Designer*, how to
open a SharePoint site in *SharePoint Designer* and how to find your way
around the user interface.

A SharePoint site can be opened locally in *SharePoint Designer*, and
when that is done you will have a good overview over the site, its
content, permissions and workflows. You can make modifications or
create a new workflow, and when you are finished the changes can be
published to the site.

You can also create a new SharePoint site and add apps and pages to it
from within *SharePoint Designer*.

Even if *SharePoint Designer* is useful for many kinds of SharePoint
enhancements and customizations, this book focuses on the workflow
possibilities given by *SharePoint Designer*.

4.1   DRAWBACKS AND BENEFITS

SharePoint Designer is a useful tool for all SharePoint administrators, but
as Microsoft has not created a 2016 version of *SharePoint Designer*, it
will probably be discontinued in the future. That is something you should
be aware of if you decide to learn and use *SharePoint Designer*.

Microsoft of course has reasons for not updating *SharePoint Designer*.
The tool is badly documented, and as it gives a possibility to get into the
SharePoint source code, users without sufficient knowledge can destroy
a SharePoint site when trying to modify it in *SharePoint Designer*.

Experienced developers have problems with *SharePoint Designer* for
another reason: it is difficult to maintain good development standards, in
SharePoint Designer.

Among the *SharePoint Designer* benefits are the data connection
possibilities, especially for SharePoint on-premise, and many no-code
solutions build on *SharePoint Designer*.

Furthermore, *SharePoint Designer* is needed if you want to create your
own workflows for SharePoint on-premises, and these workflows can of
course also be used in SharePoint Online. Workflows also give some
possibilities that are not yet present in Microsoft Flow.

4.2 TERMS

SharePoint Designer has some differences compared to SharePoint when it comes to terms.

- The synonyms "column" and "field" mean the same thing. The SharePoint web browser user interface uses the word "column", while *SharePoint Designer*, Access and the programming object models all use the word "field".

  In this book I will use "column" when I am referring to SharePoint and "field" in the *SharePoint Designer* context.

- SharePoint talks about "apps", but that concept does not exist in *SharePoint Designer*. Instead *SharePoint Designer* has lists and libraries and often only the word "list" is used for both. As a library is a kind of list that is nothing strange.

  To avoid the clumsy expression "list or library" in many places in this book, I will most often write only "lists" when I refer to common SharePoint lists as well as document libraries. Only when I want to point out that I am talking about a library specifically, I will use the word "library".

- In SharePoint we often separate files in document libraries and items in other lists, even if files also can be regarded as items. In *SharePoint Designer* the most common term is "item", and it includes files too. I follow that practice and talk about "items" in this book.

You should also know the meaning of these terms:

- The item that was created or changed and thereby triggered the workflow is called the "current item".

- Dynamic content is referred to as "lookup".

4.3 INSTALL SHAREPOINT DESIGNER 2013

SharePoint Designer 2013 SP 1 is the latest (and probably last) version of *SharePoint Designer*, and you can use it even if you have a later version of SharePoint.

SharePoint Designer 2013 is free of charge, but it is not included in any Office package installation. You will have to download and install the application. You might also want to install a Service Pack, which is downloaded from the same site as the SharePoint Designer .exe file.

NOTE: If you install Office 2016 or 2019 on a PC that already has *SharePoint Designer* 2013 installed, *SharePoint Designer* will be removed. It will still be possible to continue using *SharePoint Designer* 2013, but you must download and install it again.

4.3.1 Install from Microsoft's Download Center

To install *SharePoint Designer* 2013, go to Microsoft's Download Center at https://www.microsoft.com/download, select the Office category and find *SharePoint Designer* 2013 in the list. (The current direct link is https://www.microsoft.com/download/details.aspx?id=35491.)

Download process:

1. Click on the Download button.
2. Depending on your Office version, double-click on either the SharePointDesigner_32bit.exe file or the SharePointDesigner_64bit.exe file to start the Setup program.
3. Follow the instructions on the screen to complete the installation.

4.3.2 Install from Office 365

1. Open your Office 365 account page.
2. Click on 'Install status' and then on 'Install desktop applications'.
3. Open Tools & add-ins.
4. Under SharePoint Designer 2013, click on 'Download and install'.
5. Select language if you want another language than the default one.
6. Click on the 'Download' button.
7. Select the 32- or 64-bit version, depending on your Office version.
8. Click on 'Next'.
9. Run the file.

Demo:

https://www.kalmstrom.com/Tips/SharePoint-Workflows/SharePoint-Designer.htm

4.4 OPEN A SITE IN SHAREPOINT DESIGNER

Even if you want to work with an app, you must always open the *site* in *SharePoint Designer*.

Then, when the site is open, you can select the app you want to work with. (However, as mentioned above the concept "app" does not exist in *SharePoint Designer.* Here we have lists and libraries.)

Open Site

1. In *SharePoint Designer*, click on Open Site.

2. Paste or write in the URL of the site you want to open. Note that only the first part of the URL you see when you open the site should be entered, like this: https://kalmstromdemo.sharepoint.com/sites/Example/.

3. Click on Open.

4.5 USER INTERFACE

In *SharePoint Designer* you work with one single SharePoint site and its contents, design and settings.

When a SharePoint site is open in *SharePoint Designer*, you can see the Site Objects to the left. To the right, there is a Summary page with information about the item you have selected in the left pane.

Above the Site Objects pane and the Summary page, there is a ribbon with various controls. Which controls are displayed, depends on what has been selected in the left pane.

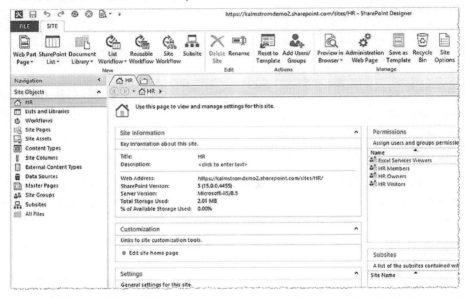

When you select the 'Workflows' entry in the left pane, the Summary page shows information about all the site's workflows: when and by whom the workflow was created and modified and what type of workflow and workflow platform it is. The ribbon shows buttons for workflow creation and management.

There are also controls in a top bar above the ribbon tabs. Use the green refresh button when you have made changes to the SharePoint site in the browser, while the site was open in *SharePoint Designer*.

Use the "preview in browser" button (to the right in the image above) when you have made changes to the SharePoint site in *SharePoint Designer* and want to see the result in the browser. You can also preview by pressing F12 on the keyboard.

The list will by default open in Internet Explorer, but you can add more browsers via the arrow to the right of the magnifying glass icon.

4.6 START CREATING A WORKFLOW

To create any type of workflow when you have opened a site in *SharePoint Designer*, select the root site or 'Workflows' in the left pane and click on one of the workflow buttons in the ribbon.

The actual conditions and actions are the same for all three kinds of workflows, but there are some differences in how you start creating them and how you set the trigger options.

In all cases, you should give the workflow a name and a description, select if it should be a SharePoint 2013 (default) or SharePoint 2010 workflow and click OK.

Now there will be a new tab in *SharePoint Designer* with the name of the workflow. Under the tab, there are two new pages: the 'Edit Workflow' page and the 'Workflow Settings' page.

The image below shows the tab for the "Notification" workflow, which is of the 2013 type. The page below is the 'Edit Workflow' page, which here shows the text-based designer.

Note: when a tab has a little star, it means that its content has not been saved.

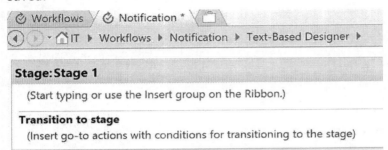

Switch between the two workflow pages with the buttons 'Edit Workflow' (visible in the Settings page ribbon) and 'Workflow Settings' (visible in the Edit page ribbon).

There is also an 'Edit workflow' link in the Workflow Settings page.

SharePoint Designer 2013 has two design views, the Text-Based Design view and the Visual Designer view, which requires Visio. In this book we will work with the Text-Based Design view for workflow creation, except for section 15.4, E-mail Alert in Visual Designer.

In the Text-Based Design view, you can find buttons for condition and action in the ribbon.

Condition Action

When you have clicked on one of these buttons, you will have this kind of link for the 'Condition' button:

If value equals value

And for the 'Action' button:

Set field to value

You build the workflow by clicking on the links to select or type in the valid values, fields or what your workflow should be using or doing.

Demo:

https://www.kalmstrom.com/Tips/SharePoint-Workflows/SPD-Overview.htm

4.7 CREATE A LIST IN SHAREPOINT DESIGNER

When you want to create a new SharePoint list and add a workflow to it, you don't have to first create the list in the browser. Instead, you can create both the list and the workflow in *SharePoint Designer*. It is quicker and saves you some clicks and loading of new pages.

1. Select 'Lists and Libraries' in the left pane.

2. Click on one of the buttons in the ribbon 'New' group.

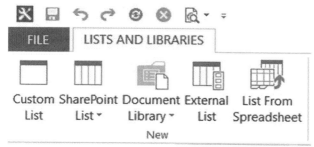

3. Give the list a name (and a description) and click OK.

Click on the new list in the summary page. Now the list options are displayed, and you can customize your list more quickly than in SharePoint. You can select setting options and add, remove and edit columns, views and forms.

Demo:

http://kalmstrom.com/Tips/SharePoint-Workflows/SharePoint-Designer-2013-Create-List.htm

5   SHAREPOINT 2010 AND 2013 WORKFLOWS

SharePoint Designer 2013 allows you to create each workflow as either a SharePoint 2010 workflow or a SharePoint 2013 workflow. The workflow platform is selected each time you start creating a new workflow. The SharePoint 2013 workflow is default.

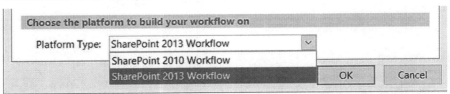

For a simple workflow, the SharePoint 2010 platform can be easier to use, but SharePoint 2013 workflows have new features that allow you to do more. Some things are however only possible with the 2010 workflow.

In most cases you can use both the 2010 and 2013 workflows, but even if I start with a few SharePoint 2010 workflows I mostly use the 2013 version for the example workflows in this book. If I don't mention the version, the process is the same for both types of workflow even if the steps are a bit different.

When an example workflow can be created with only one of the versions, I of course mention that fact.

5.1   DIFFERENCES BETWEEN 2010 AND 2013

These are the most important differences between SharePoint 2010 and SharePoint 2013 workflows:

- The SharePoint 2010 workflow is built in steps.

- The SharePoint 2013 workflow has a Stages concept, so you build the workflow in stage after stage. Each stage can hold one or more steps with actions and conditions.

  Between each stage there is a transition step, where you decide if the workflow should go to another stage or to the end of the workflow.

  You must use this transition even if the workflow only has one stage. (In that case, the transition will of course always be to go to the end of the workflow.)

> **Stage: Stage 1**
>
> (Start typing or use the Insert group on the Ribbon.)
>
> **Transition to stage**
>
> (Insert go-to actions with conditions for transitioning to the stage)

- The SharePoint 2013 workflow has another view in addition to the Text-Based Designer. It is called Visual Designer, and you can use it if you have *Microsoft Visio* installed on the same computer as *SharePoint Designer*. *Refer to* chapter 15, E-mail Alert to High Prio Assignee.

- The two most common Conditions of the SharePoint 2010 workflow have been merged into one in the SharePoint 2013 workflow.

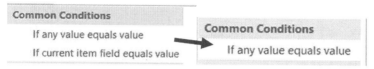

- There are more Actions in the SharePoint 2013 workflow.

- SharePoint 2010 reusable workflows can be limited to specific content types. This cannot be done with SharePoint 2013 reusable workflows, and I have yet to find a use for reusable 2013 workflows because of this limitation. *Refer to* the reusable example workflows in chapter 17, 18 and 19.

- Only SharePoint 2010 workflows can be started from a timer. *Refer to* 19.5.1, Theory: Retention Stage.

- There is no impersonation step in SharePoint 2013 workflows, and therefore there are no actions allowing you to modify permissions on items. For that, you need to use a SharePoint 2010 workflow. *Refer to* the example workflow in chapter 24, Unique Permissions.

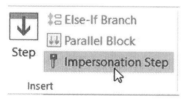

- Only SharePoint 2010 workflows can send e-mails to people outside the tenant.

- Only SharePoint 2010 workflows can declare record, *refer to* the example workflow in chapter 10.

- The SharePoint 2013 workflow can include loops. But even if loops are possible, they are hardly practicable and far beyond the scope of a "from scratch" book.

If you are interested in creating workflows with a loop, I recommend an article by Laura Rogers: https://collab365.community/call-web-service-action/.

6   WORKFLOW TYPES

A workflow can be applied to a site or a list, library or content type. If you want the workflow to be used with a content type, I recommend that you create it as a reusable workflow. A site workflow is not connected to any specific list or content type.

Below I will only describe the list workflow as a first step. We will look at the other two workflow types later in this book, in example workflows where we create such workflows.

6.1   LIST WORKFLOWS

The most common workflow is the list workflow. It is only intended to be used on the items in one list, and it cannot easily be re-used in another list. In this book I most often create the example workflows as list workflows.

6.1.1   Start Creating a List Workflow

You can start creating a list workflow in two ways:

- Select the home page or 'Workflows' in the *SharePoint Designer* left pane.

- Click on the 'List Workflow' button in the ribbon, *see* the image above. All the site's lists will be displayed in a dropdown, so that you can select the one where you want the workflow to run.

- In the left pane, open 'List and Libraries'. Then, in the summary page, open the list you want to create a workflow for and click on the New button at Workflows to start creating the new list workflow.

In both cases, the same dialog will open. Give the workflow a name and a description and select if it should be a SharePoint 2013 or SharePoint 2010 workflow.

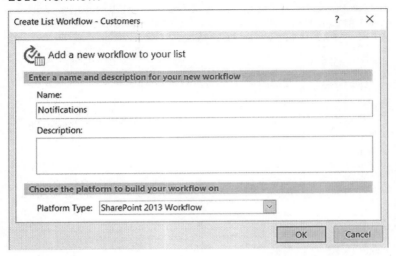

When you click OK to the creation dialog, a design page will open and you can start building the workflow.

You also need to set in *SharePoint Designer* when the workflow should be started. This is done in the Workflow Settings page. Make sure that this setting is really done, because the checking not always sticks in the box.

Start Options

Change the start options for this workflow.

☑ Allow this workflow to be manually started

☐ Start workflow automatically when an item is created

☐ Start workflow automatically when an item is changed

7   WORKFLOW TRIGGERS

A workflow must always have a trigger – something that starts the workflow. The workflow can be started manually or automatically, depending on what you want to achieve with it. A manual trigger is normally used when the workflow should be run at irregular occasions that cannot be decided in advance.

Automatic triggers are often combined with a possibility to also start the workflow manually.

SharePoint 2013 and SharePoint 2010 workflows give the same trigger options in the Workflow Settings page. Only the manual option is default.

Start Options

Change the start options for this workflow.

☑ Allow this workflow to be manually started

☐ Start workflow automatically when an item is created

☐ Start workflow automatically when an item is changed

7.1   MANUAL WORKFLOW TRIGGERS

To start a list workflow manually, you can use the link on the list's workflows page or add a button to the list.

7.1.1   Link on Workflows Page

When a workflow is created, a link to the workflow is added automatically on the list's "Workflows" page. To open the "Workflows" page for a list, right-click on an item or document and select 'More' > 'Workflow' (or 'Advanced' > 'Workflows' for the classic experience interface).

Under 'Start a New Workflow', click on the workflow you want to run. In the image below, the workflow name is "ExtractMetadata"

Start a New Workflow

ExtractMetadata

7.1.2   Start Button in the List

If you want to have a start button for the workflow in the list, this button can be created in *SharePoint Designer*. The *SharePoint Designer* button options were first intended for the classic experience interface, but they often work in the modern experience too.

- Button in the command bar:

In *SharePoint Designer*, open the list where you are using the workflow. Click on the 'Custom Action' button and select 'View Ribbon'.

Give the button a name and a description and set it to initiate the workflow. (This button can also be used to navigate to a form or an URL.)

Now a trigger command will be added in the command bar, or under the ribbon ITEM or FILE tab. Select an item to show the command in a modern list.

You can also add an image for this command in the *SharePoint Designer* Custom Action settings.

- Button in the item menu:

  Do as when creating a command bar button but select 'List Item Menu' instead of 'View Ribbon'. The trigger button will be added under the item ellipsis.

7.2   AUTOMATIC LIST WORKFLOW TRIGGERS

Both SharePoint 2013 and SharePoint 2010 workflows give these options for automatic start of a workflow:

- When an item is created.

- When an item is changed.

  Automatic triggers can be combined, so that the workflow is run when the item is created as well as when the item is changed. Most often you also want to give a possibility to start the workflow manually.

- SharePoint 2010 workflows have an additional trigger option: to set a time when the workflow should be run. This is described in 19.5, E-mail on Rental Agreement Renewal.

7.3 ACTIONS THAT START WORKFLOWS

There are some workflow actions that can start a workflow or combine an automatic start with a delay until the workflow is actually run.

7.3.1 Coordination Actions

SharePoint 2013 workflows have two 'Coordination actions' that are used to start SharePoint 2010 workflows. The 'List Workflow' option can be used for List workflows and for Reusable workflows connected to a list.

Coordination Actions
Start a List Workflow
Start a Site Workflow

7.4 WORKFLOW PERMISSIONS

Usually a workflow is run as the initiator of the trigger. That means that everything the workflow does is performed using the permissions of the initiator.

This means that if Bert creates a new item and a workflow that reacts to the "new Item is added" trigger is used in the list, all the workflow actions are performed using Bert's permissions. If the workflow tries to do something that Bert does not have enough permissions to do, the workflow will fail.

This is a common cause of trouble when writing workflows. Everything works fine when the workflow author triggers the workflow but fails when someone else runs it. To make things worse, the workflow does not notify anyone that it has failed.

There are two ways to avoid this problem:

- The obvious method is to make sure that no actions in a workflow require higher permissions than the trigger.

- Another way is to use an impersonation step, *refer to* 24.2 Theory: Impersonation Step. This step is run as the author of the workflow, but it is only present in workflows built on the SharePoint 2010 platform. If you for example want to add a loop to the workflow you cannot use this method, because loops are only possible in SharePoint 2013 workflows.

Demo:

https://www.kalmstrom.com/Tips/SharePoint-Workflows/Workflow-Triggers.htm

8   BUILD THE WORKFLOW

When a new workflow has been created in *SharePoint Designer*, it is time to start specifying what the workflow should do and when it should be done. That information is written in the workflow script.

The workflow script looks different for SharePoint 2013 and SharePoint 2010 workflows, but the principles are the same: build the script step by step with actions and conditions.

To add new content, place the mouse cursor where you want the new content to be added and click on the horizontal orange line that appears. Then click on one of the ribbon buttons to add the content, *see* the image below.

Be careful when you select the orange line, because when you move the mouse over the workflow designer, several orange lines will be visible. Make sure that you add the new content where you actually want it. If the button you want to use is greyed out, you have probably chosen the wrong place.

Indented rows show that they depend on the row above. Thus, a condition is often the first parameter you enter in a workflow script. When you add an action, which should be performed if that condition is true, the row becomes a bit indented.

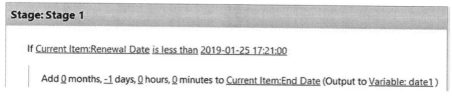

8.1   STEPS AND STAGES

Workflows are built in steps (SharePoint 2010) or stages (2013). SharePoint 2013 workflows have at least one step – the transition step – inside each stage.

The first step/stage is created automatically when you create the workflow, and a simple workflow can very well only have one step/stage.

If you want more steps/stages, place the mouse cursor where you want the new step/stage, click on the horizontal orange line that appears and then on the 'Step' or 'Stage' button in the ribbon.

Stage Step

Insert

You can also right-click on the orange line and select stage or step.

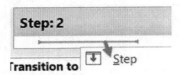

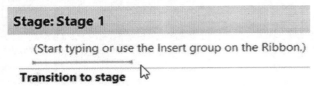

2010 workflows only have the 'Step' button, of course.

In 2013 workflows either the 'Stage' or the 'Step' button is active, depending on where you put the cursor. In the image below, from a SharePoint 2013 workflow, the orange line is visible inside a stage, and therefore the 'Step' icon is active.

Stage: Stage 1

(Start typing or use the Insert group on the Ribbon.)

Transition to stage

8.1.1   2010 Steps

SharePoint 2010 workflows are built in steps. New steps can be added inside or outside an earlier step.

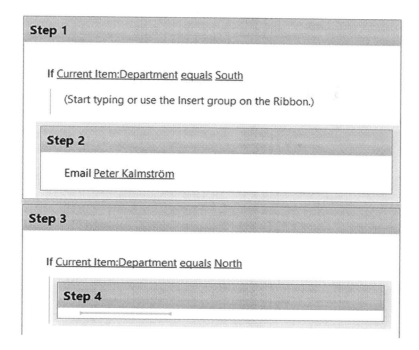

8.1.2   2013 Stages

SharePoint 2013 workflows have stages, which can contain several steps. Steps can also include other steps.

In 2013 workflows each stage must have a transition step, where you select which stage should come next. There must always be an end stage.

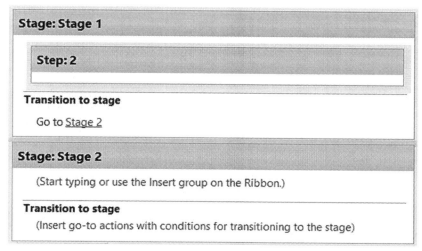

8.1.2.1 Go to the End of the Workflow

As SharePoint 2013 always must have an end stage, I usually set the end of the workflow first:

1. At 'Transition to stage', type 'go' and press Enter when you see the text 'Press Enter to insert Go to a stage'.

2. Click on a stage and select 'End of Workflow'.

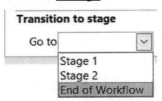

8.1.3 *Naming*

I recommend that you rename the titles of the steps and stages, so that they are easy to follow for other people who might edit the workflow. These titles are shown in the workflow status column, so it is extra important to rename the steps/stages if the status column should be visible in the default view. Also *refer to* 2.4, See Workflow Status.

Click on the step/stage name to make it possible to write and change the name.

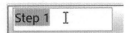

I also suggest that you use CamelCase naming or underscore in the names but not spaces when you create SharePoint lists and columns. That will give you better internal names and URLs.

Do like this to have internal CamelCase names and other names that are visible to users:

1. Create a list or a column and write the name in CamelCase style, for example "DepartmentName".

2. Save the list/column.

3. Open the list/column settings and change the name into something that is more suitable for users, for example "Department Name".

4. Now the CamelCase name will be the internal name, that you can see in the URL. In the user interface, the second name will be visible instead.

Note: In this book I have *not* renamed steps and stages that are the only one present in the workflow.

Demo:
https://www.kalmstrom.com/Tips/SharePoint-Online-Course/CamelCase-Naming.htm

8.2 ACTIONS AND CONDITIONS

Actions are the workflow building blocks that decide what the workflow should do after it has been triggered, for example send an e-mail, delete an item or even trigger another workflow.

Conditions decide when the actions should be performed. The action will be performed only if the condition is true. Each true condition can result in one or more actions.

Conditions can be followed by one action if the condition is true and another action – an Else action – if the condition is false. Insert an Else action into an existing conditional block by clicking on the 'Else Branch' button in the ribbon.

A workflow can have several conditions, where the second condition is depending on if the first condition is true and so on.

Each action and each condition has its own row in the workflow script. The actions and conditions to choose from are not quite the same in SharePoint 2010 and SharePoint 2013 workflows, but the general usage of actions and conditions in a SharePoint workflow is the same.

The workflow context decides which actions and conditions are available during the workflow creation. For details about all available conditions and actions, *refer to* information from Microsoft.

- Actions for SharePoint 2010 workflows:
  https://docs.microsoft.com/en-us/sharepoint/dev/general-development/workflow-actions-quick-reference-sharepoint-2010-workflow-platform

- Actions for SharePoint 2013 workflows:
  https://docs.microsoft.com/en-us/sharepoint/dev/general-development/workflow-actions-quick-reference-sharepoint-workflow-platform

- Conditions for SharePoint 2010 workflows:
  https://docs.microsoft.com/en-us/sharepoint/dev/general-development/workflow-conditions-quick-reference-sharepoint-2010-workflow-platform#see-also

I have not found a similar page for conditions in SharePoint 2013 workflows, but they are much the same as for the 2010 platform.

8.2.1 Add Actions and Conditions

Actions and conditions can be added to a step or stage in several ways, but you must always first select the orange line in the place where you want to add content.

- Click on the ribbon button and select the action or condition that you want to use from the dropdown.

- Right-click on the orange line to choose among the most common conditions and recent actions.

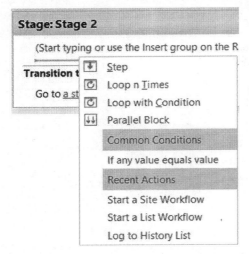

- Start writing what you want to add, and press enter when you get a good suggestion.

- Start writing what you want to add, press enter and select one of the options from the dropdown that appears.

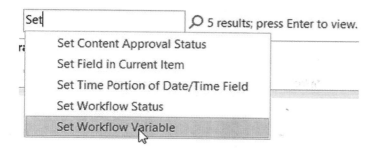

8.2.2 Specify Actions and Conditions

When you have selected an action or condition, you must specify it. Do this by clicking on the underlined text in the action or condition row. That will give you various options, and I describe some of them in the example workflows.

Demo:

https://www.kalmstrom.com/Tips/SharePoint-Workflows/Workflow-Conditions-Actions.htm

8.3 DELETE

When you select and right-click on the colored top banner of a stage or step, you will have some options on what to do with the stage/step.

Everything inside the stage/step will be affected, so be careful when you make your selection. If you, for example, want to remove a step inside a stage or step, you must make sure that you have selected only that step and not the superior stage/step.

One of the options is to delete the selected stage/step, and you can also move it up or down, copy, cut and paste. Under Advanced Properties you can rename the stage.

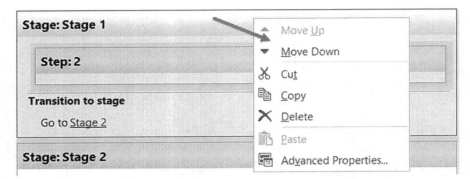

Actions and conditions can also be deleted. Click on the arrow to the right to open a dropdown that gives several options.

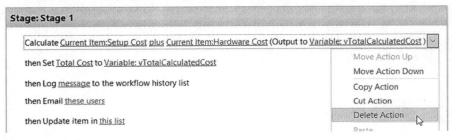

As you see in the images above there is also a copy option. In the example workflows in chapter 25, Multiple Steps Approvals, and 30, Merger Orders in a Tasks List, we make use of the copy and paste options to create new actions and stages.

Demo:

https://www.kalmstrom.com/Tips/SharePoint-Workflows/Workflow-Conditions-Actions.htm

8.4   HARD-CODED TEXT

The easiest way to decide what value a workflow parameter should have is to write it in the workflow. This is called to hard-code, because the method always gives the same result.

Hard-coding is useful if you for example want some general text in a workflow generated e-mail, like "You have received a high priority task". Then this text will be the same in all e-mails that are sent by this workflow.

But when you want to add the name of the task, or a link to it, you must use dynamic content, *see* below. If you hard-code the task name or link, the workflow can only be used for one task!

Hard-coding has a serious drawback: if a parameter value is changed, you have to modify the workflow. Therefore, you should always think twice before you hard-code.

8.5   DYNAMIC CONTENT

When you add dynamic content in a workflow, the content in actions changes depending on what happens in the SharePoint list. In *SharePoint Designer*, dynamic content is called "lookup" content, and it is added via 'Add or Change Lookup' buttons. What is shown as suggestions in the dropdowns depends on the action.

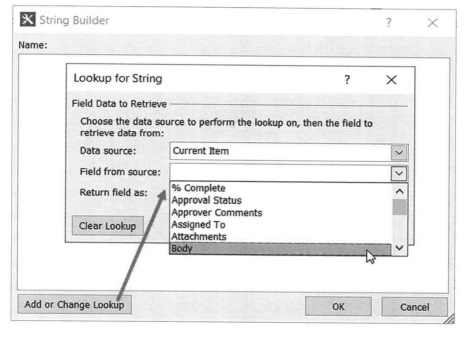

8.6   VARIABLES

A variable is like a container that holds different types of information, and you can use variables for storing, modifying and retrieving any kind of data.

The benefit of using a variable is that you can set the value of it once. Then you can reuse that variable whenever needed by adding it to the workflow via the 'Add or Change Lookup' command. (You will get to know that command later. It is used in most of the example workflows.)

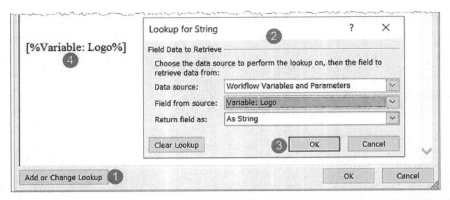

SharePoint Designer has two variable types: Initiation Form Parameters and Local Variables. Both have creation buttons in the ribbon of the workflow Edit page.

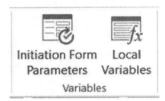

Initiation Form Parameters are used in the example workflows in chapter 24, Unique Permissions, and Local Variables are described in several example workflows from chapter 20.

8.7 CHECK, PUBLISH AND TEST THE WORKFLOW.

When you have created a workflow, you must publish it. In the same ribbon group as the 'Publish' button, you can find buttons to save the workflow (to continue working with it later) and to check the workflow for errors.

Even if you have checked the workflow for errors before you publish it, you should always control that it really works as intended. Simulate the condition described in the workflow and see if the desired action is performed.

You can see details on running and completed workflows. Right-click on an item and select 'More' or 'Advanced' and then 'Workflow' to open the Workflows page.

If you cannot check the workflow directly, because it is activated by a timer and not by a changed or created item, you can start it manually from the Workflows page.

8.7.1 Troubleshooting

Unfortunately, *SharePoint Designer* is not very good when it comes to helping users understand why workflows fail. I recommend that you build complicated workflows step by step and publish and test between each step. That way it is easier to understand where the problem is.

Sometimes it is also possible to split a long workflow into several shorter ones.

Another help in the troubleshooting is the logging.

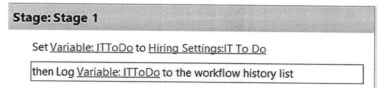

You can see the info logged by the 'Log to History List' action under Workflow History on the Workflow Status page. Users can also reach this page, so when the debugging session is complete, and the workflow is used in production, you probably want to remove the log messages.

EXAMPLE WORKFLOWS

In this section, I will give some examples on how to create useful workflows. Feel welcome to use them, or parts of them, or to just study them to understand the process.

If you are new to SharePoint workflows, I also recommend that you study the example workflows in order, because the steps are more detailed in the first examples and the workflows are more advanced later on.

I also advise you to study and preferably also create all the workflows. Even if your organization does not need all of them, you will learn a lot that you can make use of when creating your own workflows later.

To not burden the text with unnecessary information, I generally don't tell you to click OK. I assume that you understand when that should be done.

All example workflow descriptions are built in the same way:

- The **Prerequisites** sections give information about what I use in the workflow. I have given lists example names, to make the flow steps easier to follow. These names are written in italics.

  Note that I only mention what is needed for that specific workflow. For example, when I mention required SharePoint list columns, I only include those that I use in the workflow – not other columns that might be needed to make the list meaningful.

- In the **Theory** sections, I continue to give general information about *SharePoint Designer* and workflows, but I choose such knowledge that is relevant for and practiced in the example workflow at hand.

  Sometimes I also give pieces of information about SharePoint, but for general SharePoint knowledge, especially about SharePoint Online, *refer to* my book *SharePoint Online from Scratch*.

- The **Steps** build on what you have learned in the previous chapters. I will not repeat how to perform basic steps like adding an action or publishing the workflow. That would make the descriptions unnecessarily long and boring, and you can always go back to the information earlier in the book.

  Instead the Steps focus on what is special to the current example workflow, and I have tried to describe those steps in detail.

We will start with three simple SharePoint 2010 workflows, but after that I will mostly describe SharePoint 2013 workflows. These can however often be created as SharePoint 2010 workflows too.

9 ARCHIVE LIST ITEMS

SharePoint does not work well when you have more than 5000 items in a list, so it is a good idea to archive items that are no longer needed in an Archive list.

In this first example, we will create a SharePoint 2010 workflow that copies closed items from one list to another and then deletes the copied items from the original list.

9.1 PREREQUISITES

A *HelpDesk* list, built on the tasks template. It has an "Issue Status" Choice column where one of the options is "Closed".

The *HelpDesk* list is saved as a template (in the SharePoint list settings), and this template is used to create a new list, *ArchiveHelpDesk*. Make sure that the 'Include Content' box is unchecked (default) when you create the template.

9.2 THEORY: SELECT WORKFLOW OPTIONS

In this first example workflow, we will use the condition 'If current item field equals value'.

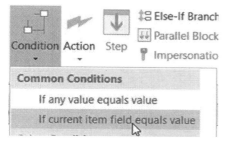

When you have added this condition to the workflow, it looks like this:

If field equals value

The underlined parameters field and value are blue, and you must click on them to set the desired value.

The parameter equals is also underlined, but it is black. This means that you can either leave the parameter as it is or click on it to select another value.

You must define the parameters in sequence, from left to right, because the options for the second and third parameter depend on what the first value in the condition is set to.

We will also use two actions in this example workflow: 'Copy List Item' and 'Delete Item'. They work in the same way: click on underlined text to define a value. The 'Copy List Item' action only exists on the SharePoint 2010 platform, so therefore we must use that workflow type.

NOTE: the item's version history is lost when you archive this way, so you should not archive list items until you know that you don't need their earlier versions.

9.3 STEPS

This workflow runs when an item in the *HelpDesk* list is changed. It first checks if the item that triggered the workflow (= the item that was changed) has the "Issue Status" column set to 'Closed'.

If that condition is true, the workflow first copies the item to the *ArchiveHelpDesk* list and then deletes it from the *HelpDesk* list. Skip step 4 if you want to keep the closed items in both lists.

1. Create a new SharePoint 2010 list workflow for the *HelpDesk* list. Give the workflow a name (and a description).

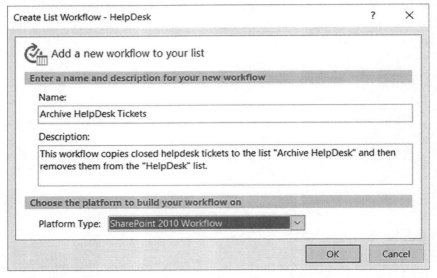

2. Add the condition 'If current item field equals value':

    a. Click on <u>field</u> and select 'Issue Status' from the dropdown.

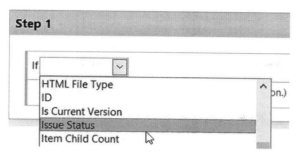

b. Keep <u>equals</u> as it is and click on <u>value</u>.

c. Select 'Closed' from the dropdown.

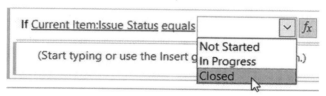

3. Add the action 'Copy List Item':

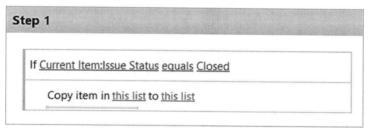

a. Click on the first <u>this list</u> and click OK to the default Current Item.

b. Click on the second <u>this list</u> and select the *ArchiveHelpDesk* list.

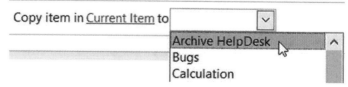

4. Add the action 'Delete Item'. Click on <u>this list</u> and click OK to the default Current Item. (Be sure to add this action inside the condition, as in the image below.)

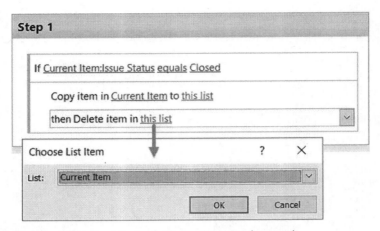

5. Set the workflow to start when an item is changed.

6. Check and publish the workflow.

7. Test the workflow by closing a dummy item or an item that should be closed anyway in the *HelpDesk* list. Make sure the item is moved to the *ArchiveHelpDesk* list and deleted from the *HelpDesk* list.

Demo:

https://www.kalmstrom.com/Tips/SharePoint-Workflows/Archive-SharePoint-List-Items.htm

10 DECLARE RECORD WORKFLOW

When you want to protect a SharePoint item, you can declare it "record", which means that you put certain restrictions on the item that are not tied to permissions. Most often you want to protect library documents from being edited or deleted.

Instead of declaring record manually, to protect SharePoint list items, you can use a workflow that automatically declares an item record if a certain condition is met. Such a workflow is very easily created, when you have a policy for which items should be declared record.

Here we imagine a SharePoint document library for CV files that should be declared record when a decision about the applicant is made.

10.1 PREREQUISITES

A SharePoint document library called "CVs". It has a Choice column for "Status" with the three options "Under Review" (default), "Employed" and "Rejected".

The files in the library should be declared record when a decision is made – that is, when the "Status" value is changed into "Employed" or "Rejected".

Before you start creating this workflow, make sure that the declare records feature is activated for the site collection.

10.2 THEORY: NOT EQUALS

In this example workflow, we use the list action 'Declare Record', which is only available for SharePoint 2010 workflows.

The action 'Declare Record' depends on the same condition as in the previous example workflow: 'If current item field equals value'. However, here we will select the 'not equals' option. This option will exclude only one option and make the condition true for all other options.

10.3 STEPS

The workflow first checks if the "Status" column has the value "Under Review" or not. If the column has another value, the file is declared record.

1. Create a SharePoint 2010 list workflow for the "CVs" library.

2. Add the condition 'If current item field equals value':

   a. Click on field and select "Status" from the dropdown.

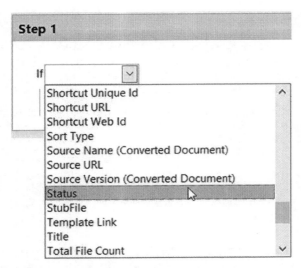

b. Click on equals and select 'not equals'.

c. Click on value and select 'Under Review'.

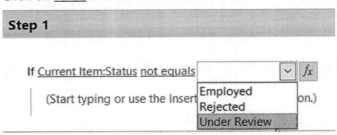

3. Add the action 'Declare record'.

4. Set the workflow to start when an item is created or changed.

5. Check, publish and test the workflow.

Demo:

http://www.kalmstrom.com/Tips/SharePoint-Workflows/Declare-Record-Workflow.htm

11 E-MAIL ALERT WHEN AN ITEM IS CHANGED

This is a continuation on what I wrote in section 3.5 about change alerts. "If you, for example, want to customize the body of the e-mail that is sent out, you must let it be generated by a workflow."

In this first example workflow, we will however not include the body. Instead, I will describe how you can let a workflow send an e-mail similar to the built-in ones. That way you will learn the basics, and later you can expand this workflow as you like.

11.1 PREREQUISITES

A SharePoint library.

11.2 THEORY: TO AND SUBJECT

In this example workflow, you will learn to specify details in the 'To' and 'Subject' fields of an auto-generated e-mail.

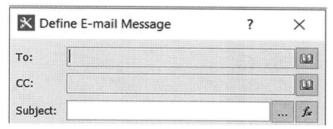

You cannot write an e-mail address directly in the 'To' field when you define the details in a workflow generated e-mail. Instead, click on the Address Book icon to the right of the field to open The Select Users dialog. Here you have a lot of options, and recently used names are also suggested.

In this example, we are using the creator of the item as the receiver of the change alert, but you can also just type in the name or e-mail address for the person or group that should receive the e-mail in the Select Users dialog.

Another option is to choose 'People/Groups from SharePoint site…' to have a selection when you click on the 'Add' button. Now you can search for specific people or groups.

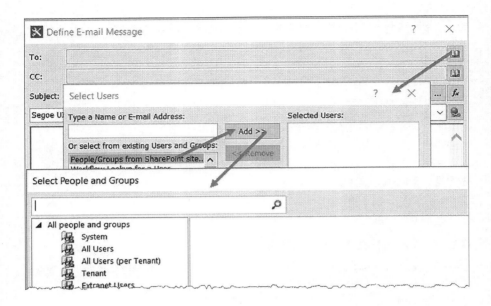

You can also use a lookup from another list.

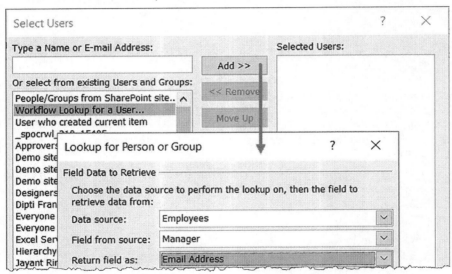

It is possible to write in the 'Subject' field, so you can just type a suitable subject.

If you want to add a Lookup for dynamic content instead of text, you can use the Function Builder. Use the String Builder when you want to add both hard-coded text and one or more Lookups for dynamic content in the subject. Both these Builders are described in 13.4, Theory: String and Function Builders.

11.3 STEPS

With this workflow, the creator gets an e-mail when someone changes an item that he/she has created.

Note that the steps are for a SharePoint 2013 workflow, so we need to go to the end of the workflow, *refer to* 5.1, Differences between 2010 and 2013.

1. Create a new list workflow for a library.

2. Go to the end of the workflow.

3. Add the action 'Send an e-mail':

   a. Add the receiver of the e-mail:

      i. Click on <u>these users</u>.

      ii. Click on the lookup icon to the right of the 'To' field.

      iii. Select 'User who created current item'.

      iv. Click on 'Add'.

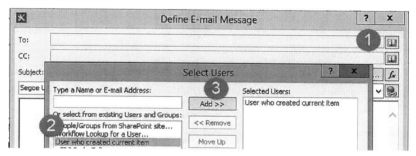

   b. Add a subject:

      i. Open the String Builder by clicking on the ellipsis to the right of the subject field.

      ii. Click on 'Add or Change Lookup' to add a lookup for the Name of the current item.

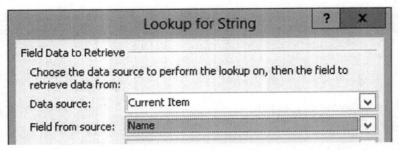

iii. Click OK to add the dynamic content to the String Builder and add suitable text.

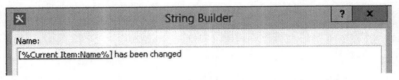

iv. Click OK to add the string to the subject.

4. Set the workflow to when an item is changed under 'Start Options' in the Workflow settings.

5. Check, publish and test the workflow.

This workflow was a simple first try, but you can expand by adding more dynamic content in the body. You will learn more about that in later example workflows.

Demo:

https://www.kalmstrom.com/Tips/SharePoint2013ChangeAlerts.htm (last part)

12 ALERT E-MAIL TO ASSIGNED WITH CC

This example list workflow sends an e-mail to the assignee and a sales manager, when an item has been created in a task list.

You can use this kind of workflow for any people/group and any SharePoint list. You can also let the workflow send the e-mail when an item has been changed.

12.1 PREREQUISITES

A SharePoint list called "Sales Tasks" with a Person or Group type column, here called "Sales Manager".

12.2 THEORY: PERSON OR GROUP COLUMNS

When you use a list with a 'Person or Group' column in a workflow, the workflow automatically gets a number of properties from the user object, such as department and e-mail address. That information can of course be very useful in the workflow.

Here we use the account information to have the e-mail addresses of the assignee and the cc. These people need to have an account in the farm or tenant. Otherwise you cannot use the 'Person or Group' column at all.

12.3 STEPS

This workflow is nearly like the previous one. I have just added a cc e-mail address.

1. Create a list workflow for the "Sales Tasks" list.

2. Set the 'Transition to Stage' to 'Go to End of Workflow'.

3. Add the action 'Send an Email':

   a. Click on these users.

   b. For To, click on the Address Book icon to the right of the 'To' field.

      i. Select 'Workflow Lookup for a User' in the Define E-mail Message dialog.

      ii. Click on 'Add' and select Field from source: 'Assigned To' and Return field as: 'Email Address'.

c. For CC, click on the Address Book icon to the right of the 'CC' field.

    i. Select 'Workflow Lookup for a User' in the Define E-mail Message dialog.

    ii. Click on 'Add' and select 'Sales Manager' and 'Email Address' in the Lookup dialog.

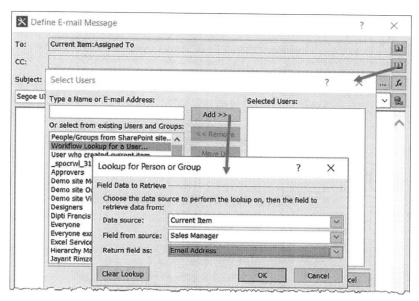

d. Enter a subject and the e-mail body text.

e. (You can also add a lookup for the title of the task and a link to the item that opens in edit mode; *refer to* 15.3.1, Link to Item in Edit Mode.)

f. Check, publish and test the workflow.

Demo:

http://kalmstrom.com/Tips/SharePoint-Workflows/HelpDesk-Notify-Boss.htm

13   ENFORCE A BUSINESS RULE

To enforce a business rule in a SharePoint list, you can let a workflow both undo the forbidden action and send an automatic e-mail to the user who tried to do something that was against the rule.

This example workflow reacts by rolling back the value in a 'Task Status' column to 'In Progress' if a user sets the column to 'Completed' without filling out the 'Minutes worked' column.

The workflow also sends a reminder e-mail to the user who tried to complete a task without entering a "Minutes worked" value. The e-mail contains a link to the task and information that the field must be filled out.

13.1   PREREQUISITES

A SharePoint *IT Tasks* list built on the Tasks template. It has a mandatory, custom Number column, "Minutes worked", where the default value is '0'.

13.2   SHAREPOINT MANDATORY COLUMN AND CHECKBOX CONFLICT

The SharePoint Tasks template gives a checkbox for task completion in the default view. When it is checked, the task is crossed out and the value in the '% Completed' column is automatically set to 100 – which in turn sets the 'Completed' column to 'Yes'.

☑   ~~Send monthly invoices~~

When you have a mandatory column, like "Minutes worked" in this example, you of course want to force users to fill it out. But the list setting 'Require that this column contains information' only prevents users from save the item without filling out the mandatory column.

However, as users can check the Completed box without opening the item, a task can be closed even if a mandatory column is not filled out. This example workflow solves that problem.

(Another problem with making the column mandatory, is that it always applies. Forcing users to fill out the number of minutes it took to complete a task before it is done, will probably result in bad data.)

13.3   THEORY: UPDATE LIST ITEM

In this example we will use two instances of the most common SharePoint 2013 condition: 'If any value equals value'. Both must be true for the action to take place.

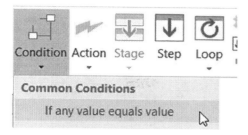

The action is 'Update List Item'. Like most of the other actions and conditions, it works through underlined text that you click on to specify the value you want the workflow to look for.

In the Update List Item dialog, you can select any list in the current SharePoint site – or the current item in the list you created the workflow for. Then click on 'Add' to select field and value.

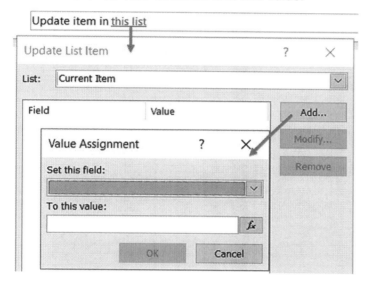

13.4 THEORY: STRING AND FUNCTION BUILDERS

In this workflow, and in all the following example workflows, we will make use of two "Builders", for strings and for functions.

13.4.1.1 String Builder

A string is a sequence of characters, either a literal constant or a variable. Open the String Builder by clicking on an ellipsis button to the right of an empty field.

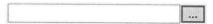

A String Builder dialog will open, where you can add text and dynamic content, called lookups in *SharePoint Designer*.

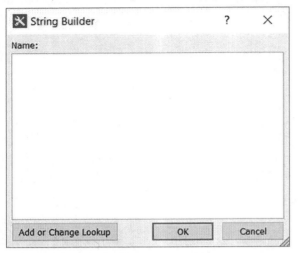

When you click OK, the string you have built will be added to the field to the left of the ellipsis icon.

13.4.2 Function Builder

Open the Function Builder by clicking on the function icon to the right of an empty field.

In *SharePoint Designer* workflows, functions are created in Lookup dialogs.

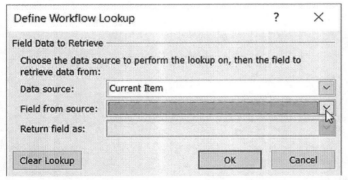

Select a data source and then a field from that source and decide how the field should be returned, when there are several options. If the data returned from the function has only one possible format, 'Return field as' is not active.

When you click OK, the function you have built will be added to the field to the left of the function icon.

13.5 STEPS

This workflow runs when an item is changed. It first checks if the 'Task Status' column is set to 'Completed' and then if the 'Minutes worked' is set to '0'.

If both these conditions are true, the workflow will update the list item and set the 'Task Status' column to 'In Progress'.

If both conditions are true, the workflow will also send an e-mail to the person who modified the task and point out that the 'Minutes worked' must be filled out. That e-mail body has a link to the item.

1. Create a list workflow for the *IT Tasks* list.

2. Go to the end of the workflow.

3. Add the condition 'If any value equals value':

   a. Click on the first <u>value</u> and open the Function Builder. Set the value to 'Current Item' >'Task Status'.

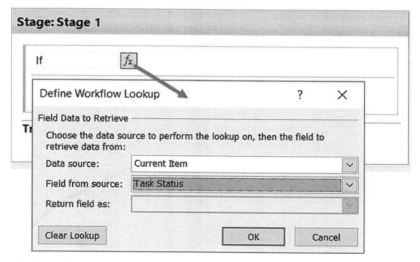

   b. Click on the second <u>value</u> and select 'Completed' from the dropdown.

4. Add another Condition 'If any value equals value' inside the first Condition and set the first <u>value</u> to 'Current Item' >'Minutes worked' in the Function Builder.

5. Write in '0' instead of the second <u>value</u>. (When you click outside the Condition, '0' will become '0.0'.)

Stage: Stage 1

If <u>Current Item:Task Status</u> <u>equals</u> <u>Completed</u>

<u>and</u> <u>Current Item:Minutes worked</u> <u>equals</u> <u>0.0</u>

6. Add the Action 'Update List Item':

   a. Click on <u>this list</u>.

   b. Keep 'Current Item' and click on 'Add'.

   c. Select the 'Task Status' field and the value 'In Progress'.

7. Add the Action 'Send an Email':

   a. Click on <u>these users</u>.

b. Open the Address Book at 'To'.

c. Select 'Workflow Lookup for a User' and click on 'Add'.

d. Keep 'Current Item' and select 'Modified By' >'Email Address'.

e. Open the String Builder at 'Subject':

f. Write in the text "You need to fill out Minutes worked for" + a Lookup for the task name.

g. In the e-mail body, click on the hyperlink icon.

h. Write the anchor text "Click here to reach the task" and add a Lookup for 'Workflow Context' >'Current Item URL'.

8. Set the workflow to start automatically when an item is changed.

9. Check, publish and test the workflow.

Here we have just added a link to the task in the e-mail body, but if you want it to be even easier for the user to correct the mistake you can let the link open the task in edit mode. *Refer to* 15.3.1 Theory: Link to Item in Edit Mode.

Demo:

http://www.kalmstrom.com/Tips/SharePoint-Workflows/Enforce-Business-Rule.htm

14 ROLL BACK COLUMN CHANGES

If you want to make sure that a SharePoint column values stays the same, you can use a workflow that reacts to changes. Here I suggest two workflows for a rollback process: first one that sets the original column value and then one that rolls back any changes.

I recommend that you enable Version history in the *Departments* list (List settings >Versioning settings), so that you can see if any changes have been made. Even if they are rolled back by the workflow, they will still be visible in the Version history.

If you want to expand this workflow and repeat techniques shown in earlier examples, you can add a send email action which informs the person who changed the department name why department name changes are not allowed.

14.1 PREREQUISITES

A SharePoint *Departments* list with these columns:

- The 'Title' column has been renamed to "Department Name".
- A Single line of text column, "Original Department Name". This column should be hidden from the view when the workflow has been finalized.

14.2 THEORY: MULTIPLE WORKFLOWS IN ONE LIST

Generally, I maintain that having multiple workflows is preferable to having one big workflow with many stages, steps, conditions and actions. Also, I recommend against having long-running workflows. It is technically possible to have workflows that run for months or even years, but it becomes difficult to handle business rule changes and SharePoint changes in those time frames.

However, it can also be complicated to have multiple workflows active on one list. They can interfere with each other, trigger each other and it is also difficult to determine the sequence of workflows, which workflow runs first after a trigger.

Here I will show an example of how it can be necessary to have two workflows in the same list to achieve a goal. We use one workflow that runs at creation of a new item and another workflow that runs at item change, and therefore they will not interfere with each other.

14.3 STEPS

To protect the values in the "Department Name" column, we will use two workflows:

- We start by creating a workflow that sets the original value for the newly created item that triggered the workflow. This original value is set by updating the list so that the "Original Department Name" column gets the same value as the "Department Name" column.

- After that, we will create the actual rollback workflow that is triggered when an item is changed. This workflow first checks the two columns to see if the values are equal or not. If they are different, the workflow updates the item and sets the value in the "Department Name" column to the same as in the "Original Department Name" column.

Set original value:

1. Create a list workflow for the *Departments* list.

2. Go to the end of the workflow.

3. Add the action 'Update List Item':

    a. Click on this list.

    b. Keep the default 'Current Item' and click on 'Add'.

    c. In the Value Assignment dialog, select 'Original Department Name'.

    d. Click on the Function Builder icon to set the value.

    e. Keep the default 'Current Item' and set the field to 'Department Name'.

4. Set the workflow to start when an item is created.

5. Check, publish and test the workflow.

Roll-back name changes:

1. Create another list workflow for the *Departments* list.

2. Go to the end of the workflow.

3. Add the condition 'If any value equals value'.

   a. Click on the first <u>value</u> and then on the Function Builder icon.

   b. Keep the default source 'Current Item' and set the field to 'Original Department Name'.

c. Click on 'equals' and select 'not equals'.

d. Click on the second <u>value</u> and then on the Function Builder icon.

e. Keep the default source 'Current Item' and set the Field to 'Department Name'.

4. Add the action 'Update List Item':

a. Click on <u>this list</u>.

b. Keep the default 'Current Item' and click on 'Add'.

c. In the Value Assignment dialog, select 'Department Name'.

d. Click on the Function Builder icon to set the value.

e. Keep the default 'Current Item' and set the field to 'Original Department Name'.

5. Set the workflow to start when an item is changed.

6. Check, publish and test the workflow.

Demo:

https://www.kalmstrom.com//Tips/SharePoint-Workflows/WF-Rollback.htm

15 E-MAIL ALERT TO HIGH PRIO ASSIGNEE

We will now create another example workflow that sends an e-mail alert to the person who has been assigned a task, but this workflow will only run when the new task has high priority. We will create this workflow in two ways, in the two different design views that are present for SharePoint 2013 workflows.

15.1 PREREQUISITES

A SharePoint tasks list or another list that has "Assigned To" and "Priority" columns.

15.2 THEORY: THE 2013 DESIGN VIEWS

The most common workflow designer is the Text-Based one, and that is the designer I have described earlier in the book.

The SharePoint 2010 workflow only has the Text-Based Designer, but SharePoint 2013 workflows also have a Visual Designer view. Here you can create workflows by dragging shapes to a design surface.

Select view in the ribbon of the SharePoint 2013 workflows. The Text-Based Designer is default.

I use the Text-Based Designer in the example workflows in this book, but I still wanted to show how the Visual Designer can be used. As a comparison, I start with creating this example workflow in the Text-Based Designer. After that I will create a similar workflow in the Visual Designer.

15.3 E-MAIL ALERT IN TEXT-BASED DESIGNER

You will recognize most workflow steps in this example, but the e-mail body link to the current item in edit mode is new.

15.3.1 Theory: Link to Item in Edit Mode

In workflows that send an e-mail when an item is created or changed, it is often necessary for the receiver to do something with the item. In those cases, it is convenient if the e-mail body has a link to the item's edit form.

To link to the current item's edit form, you first have to get the link to the list edit form. This is best done in *SharePoint Designer*:

1. Click on 'All Files' in the left pane.

2. Click on 'Lists'.

3. Click on the list that you are using in the workflow. That will give you a number of ASPX pages.

4. Right-click on EditForm.aspx and select Properties.

5. Select the full link.

6. Right-click on the link and select 'Copy'.

7. Make the URL point to the current item:

   a. Create the workflow. When you define the e-mail, paste the edit form URL in the e-mail body String Builder.

   b. After EditForm.aspx, add "?ID=" + a lookup for the ID of the current item.

The URL will turn out like this:

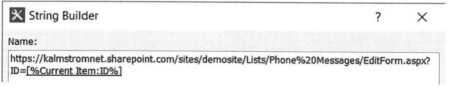

In all example workflows where I just link to the item in standard mode, you can of course replace those steps with the steps for the item in edit mode – and vice versa!

Demo:

http://kalmstrom.com/Tips/SharePoint-Workflows/HelpDesk-Direct-Link.htm

15.3.2 *Steps*

The workflow first checks if the Priority field in the newly created item has the value 'High'. If that condition is true, the workflow sends an e-mail to the assignee.

1. Create a new list workflow for the tasks list.

2. Go to the end of the workflow.

3. Add the Condition 'If any value equals value'.

   a. Click on the first <u>value</u> and then on the Function Builder icon.

   b. Keep Current Item and set the field to 'Priority'.

   c. Click on the second <u>value</u> and select 'High' from the dropdown.

4. Add the action 'Send an Email':

   a. Click on <u>these users</u>.

   b. Click on the To Address Book icon and select 'Workflow Lookup for a User' in the dialog.

   c. Click on 'Add' and select 'Assigned To' and 'Email Address'.

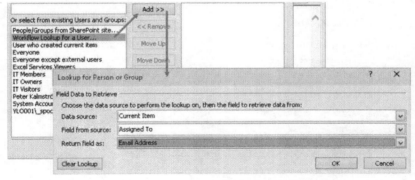

   d. Click on the subject ellipsis to open the String Builder.

   e. Enter a hard-coded subject text and add a lookup for the 'Title' of the high priority item.

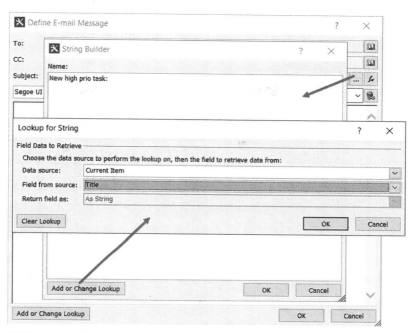

f. Write some hard-coded body text.

g. Select the body text that you want to link and click on the hyperlink icon.

h. Paste the EditForm.aspx URL into the 'Address' field in the Edit Hyperlink dialog.

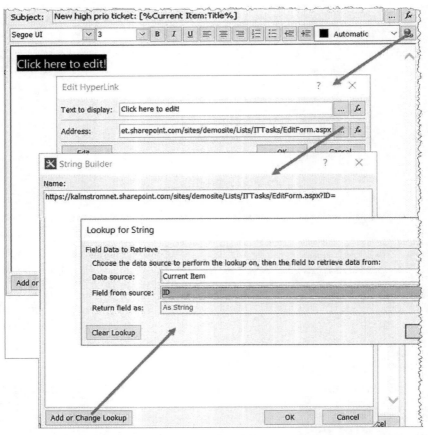

i. Click on the ellipsis to the right of the 'Address' field

j. Add "?ID=" to the EditForm.aspx URL in the String Builder.

k. Add a lookup for the ID of the current item after "?ID=".

5. Set the workflow to start when an item is created or changed.

6. Check, publish and test the workflow.

This is the finished workflow stage:

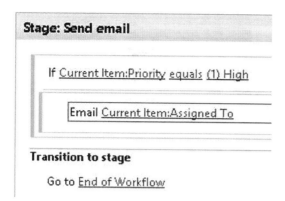

Demo:

http://kalmstrom.com/Tips/SharePoint-Workflows/HelpDesk-
Notification-2013-Workflow.htm

15.4 E-MAIL ALERT IN VISUAL DESIGNER

Now I will describe a similar workflow as above, created in the Visual
Designer View.

15.4.1 Theory: Visual Designer View

SharePoint Designer 2013 has a Visual Designer view for SharePoint
2013 workflows. Here you can create a workflow by dragging shapes to
a design surface.

You can also create your workflow in the Text-Based Designer and then
open it in the Visual Designer view. The workflow will then render into a
Visio presentation that you, for example, can show when explaining the
workflow to a customer.

You must have the 2013 version of either the Enterprise or the Architect
edition of Visio installed on the same PC as *SharePoint Designer* 2013 to
use the Visual Designer view. (Visio 2016 does not support this view.)
This is a paid Microsoft application, so all readers of this book do not
have it. That is the reason I only show one example workflow with the
Visual Designer. However, if you have Visio installed and prefer the
Visual Designer, I am sure you can follow the steps in my example
workflows in that design view also.

If you are not used to reading code, the Visual Designer view might be
easier to understand and explain than the Text-Based Designer. You can
write your own text in the Visual Designer shapes, and Visual Designer
gives a picture that describes the conditions and actions.

85

The image below shows the design surface when the workflow is finished: If the item is high prio – Yes, send notification and then go to the end of the workflow. If the item is not high prio – do not send a notification but go directly to the end.

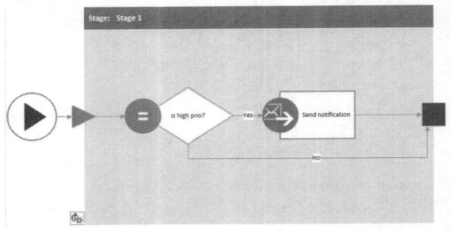

15.4.2 Steps

1. Start Visio before you begin working in SharePoint Designer.

2. Create a new list workflow for the tasks list.

3. Give the new workflow a name and a description and keep the default platform type, SharePoint 2013 workflow.

4. Click on the View button in the ribbon and select Visual Designer. Visio will now open inside SharePoint Designer.

5. Under 'Shapes' in the left pane, click on 'Conditions' and then drag the shape 'If any value equals value' to the design surface as the first stage.

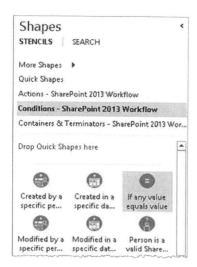

6. Click on the gearwheel icon and select Value.

7. Select Assigned To and then High.

8. Under 'Shapes' in the left pane, click on 'Actions' and then drag the shape 'Send an email' to the design surface and place it after the first shape you added.

9. Click on the gearwheel icon and select 'Email'.

10. Click on <u>these users</u> and select 'Workflow Lookup for a User'.

11. Click on 'Add' and select the 'Field from source' Assigned To and the 'Return field as' Email Address.

12. Enter a subject for the e-mail to be sent and add the body text you wish to use.

13. To connect the Condition shape and the Action shape, Right-click on the connector between them and select Yes.

14. Select the Condition shape to show the Connector tool in the ribbon and create another connection from the Condition to the end of the workflow. Right-click on the connector and select No.

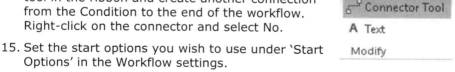

15. Set the start options you wish to use under 'Start Options' in the Workflow settings.

16. Check, publish and test the workflow.

Demo:

http://kalmstrom.com/Tips/SharePoint-Workflows/HelpDesk-Workflow-Visual-Designer.htm

16 VERSION HISTORY LINK

Version History is a SharePoint feature that makes it possible to see and restore earlier versions of items and files. The Version History also shows who made the changes to the document and when the change was done.

Version History is enabled by default in SharePoint document libraries. To reach it, select a file, click on the ellipsis at the item and select 'Version History'. Modern apps also have a 'Version history' link in the command bar ellipsis.

In this example workflow, we will add icons that link to each new file's Version History in a SharePoint document library. It is not difficult to understand if you have some knowledge about HTML code, but I hope you can follow the steps even without that knowledge.

Procedures

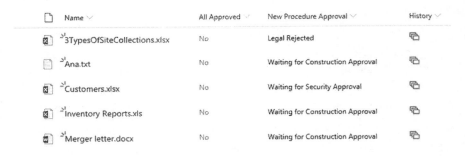

	Name ⌄	All Approved ⌄	New Procedure Approval ⌄	History ⌄
📄	3TypesOfSiteCollections.xlsx	No	Legal Rejected	🗐
📄	Ana.txt	No	Waiting for Construction Approval	🗐
📄	Customers.xlsx	No	Waiting for Security Approval	🗐
📄	Inventory Reports.xls	No	Waiting for Construction Approval	🗐
📄	Merger letter.docx	No	Waiting for Construction Approval	🗐

Similar buttons can of course be used for other things than the Version History. They can for example point to another web-based system, like a customer page in a CRM system, a map coordinate or a Power BI report. In fact, adding a relevant link to a list item can be a powerful, user-friendly and cheap way to integrate systems. (Systems integrations are often extremely difficult and costly.)

16.1 PREREQUISITES:

- A SharePoint library, here called *Procedures*. It has a custom Multiple lines of text "History" column where enhanced rich text is enabled. (*Refer to* Theory below on how to create such a column.)

- An icon, placed in the Site Assets library in the same site as the *Procedures* library.

16.2 THEORY: ADD ENHANCED RICH TEXT IN LIBRARIES

SharePoint gives a possibility to add enhanced rich text to multiple lines of text columns, but if you create the new column in SharePoint, you can only get the rich text in lists, not in libraries. To have a multiple lines of text column with enhanced rich text in a library, you must create it in *SharePoint Designer*:

1. Select 'Lists and Libraries' in the left pane.

2. Click on the library where you want to add the new column to open its summary page.

3. Click on 'Edit Columns' in the ribbon.

4. Click on the 'Add New Column' button in the ribbon.

5. Select the 'Multi Lines of Text' option from the dropdown.

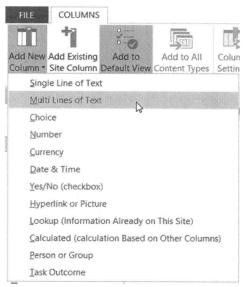

6. Click once on 'NewColumn1' and give the new column a more appropriate name.

7. Double-click on the column row to show the properties.

8. Check the box for 'Enhanced Rich Text'. You can also add information that the field will be filled out by a workflow in the Description.

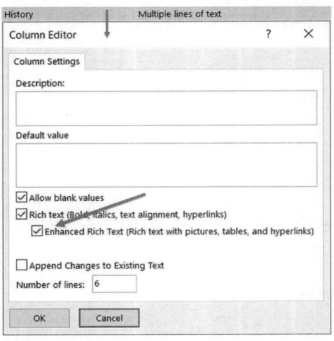

9. Click OK and Save.

16.3 STEPS

This workflow adds a Version History link in each new item's "History" column with an "Update List Item" action. The link is built from the current site URL, the list ID and a lookup for the ID of the current item.

You can get the list ID by going into the library settings and copy the last part of the URL, after 'List='.

ayouts/15/listedit.aspx?List=%7B6621b54b-4739-4827-859a-eebd9229657c%7D

This part can be used as it is, but as it is encoded it is difficult to understand. There are online decoders that give a nicer list ID that is easier to grasp.

1. Create a list workflow for the *Procedures* library.

2. Go to the end of the workflow.

3. Add the Action 'Update Item':

   a. Click on 'this list' and keep the Current Item.

   b. Click on 'Add' and select the "History" field.

   c. Open the String Builder to set the value. It will be a linked image like this: (Add your own values instead of the bold text.)

      <a href="

      [%Workflow Context:Current Site URL%]_layouts/15/Versions.aspx?list=**LISTID**&ID[%Current Item ID%]" target="_blank"><img src="**IMAGEURL**"></a>

      i. Start writing the link: <a href="

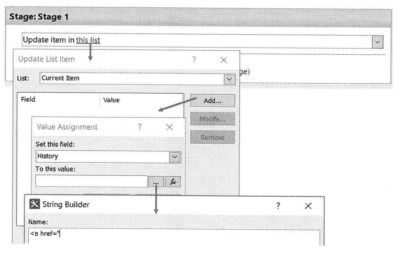

ii. Add a lookup for the Site URL by selecting first 'Workflow Context' and then 'Current Site URL'

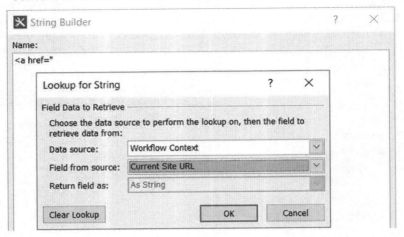

iii. Add _layouts/15/Versions.aspx?list=

iv. Add the list ID.

v. To get the current item, add &ID= and then a lookup for the Current Item ID.

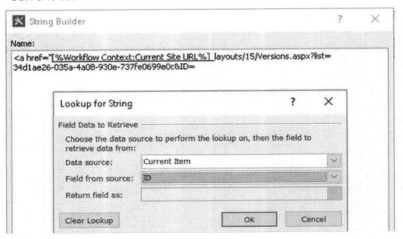

vi. Add a citation mark to finish the href.

vii. To get the link to open in a new tab, add target="_blank" before you finish the link with >.

viii. Start adding the image link: <img src="

ix. In the Site Assets, right-click on the image to get its link. Paste the link and add "> to finish the src.

x. Finish the image anchor with </a>.

Name:

```
<a href="[%Workflow Context:Current Site URL%] layouts/15/Versions.aspx?list=
34d1ae26-035a-4a08-930e-737fe0699e0c&ID=[%Current Item:ID%]" target="_blank"><img
src="https://kdemo27.sharepoint.com/sites/HQ/SiteAssets/VH.png"></a>
```

4. Set the workflow to start automatically when an item is created or changed.

5. Check, publish and test the workflow.

16.3.1 Update Existing Files

Even if the workflow is run at both change and creation, existing files that are not touched will still miss the Version History link. A quick way to make the workflow run on existing files, is to create a temporary column in the library and set a value that changes the metadata of all items.

1. Create a new single line of text column.

2. Edit the view to show the Title column and the new column.

3. Open the library in Quick Edit mode and enter any value in the first cell of the new column.

4. Fill the value down to all documents. This will change all items and thus trigger the workflow to run. (If you have many files in the library, you can do this better in Access.)

5. When the workflow has run, and all the documents are updated, remove the temporary column again.

Demo:

https://www.kalmstrom.com/Tips/SharePoint-Workflows/Version-History-Link.htm

17 SET TITLE WORKFLOWS

The SharePoint Search displays title hits on top, so for the search to work well it is important that title columns in lists and libraries are filled out with terms that give relevant information.

In SharePoint lists, it is mandatory to fill out the title, and that is a good reason for re-naming that column instead of creating a new column for important information.

In SharePoint document libraries, however, users often don't enter anything in the title field, and that has several reasons.

- The title field is not mandatory in libraries.

- The title does not have the same importance in a file system as it has in SharePoint, so files that are imported into SharePoint libraries will often lack titles or have irrelevant titles.

- When you create a new SharePoint library, the title column is not visible by default.

This example workflow does something about the title issue in SharePoint document libraries, because it gives the title column in each item the same value as the document name.

Just like in chapter 15, we will create two workflows that do the same thing. This time we will only use the Text-Based designer, but we will create one list workflow and one reusable workflow.

17.1 PREREQUISITES

A SharePoint document library with the default "Document" content type.

17.2 THEORY: TRIGGER POSSIBILITIES

I suggest two trigger possibilities for this flow: "When an item is created or changed" for existing SharePoint document libraries and only "When an item is created" for new libraries.

By checking the box also for the "changed" option, it is easy to update all files in existing libraries by modifying all of them at the same time in edit mode, *refer to* 16.3.1 Update Existing Files. However, if you keep that trigger, users cannot set another title than the document name even if they want to. Any later, manual title changes will be revoked by the workflow.

With just a "created" trigger for new libraries, the workflow will set the title to the same as the name for all new files, but the workflow will not run when files are modified. Therefore, you can change any titles manually, into something else than the name value, without having the workflow thwart your modification.

17.3 LIST WORKFLOW TO SET TITLE

The list workflow described here is easy to create, but it is directly connected to just one list. If you want to set the title to the same as the name in another list, you must re-create the workflow for that list too.

The workflow first checks if the 'Title' value is the same as the file name. If this is not true, the workflow sets the 'Title' field to the same value as the 'Name' field.

1. Create a list workflow for the library.

2. Go to the end of the workflow.

3. Add the Condition 'If any value equals value':

    a. Click on the first <u>value</u> and open the Function Builder.

    b. Keep Current Item and set the field to 'Title'.

    c. Click on <u>equals</u> and select 'not equals' from the dropdown.

    d. Click on the second <u>value</u> and open the Function Builder.

    e. Keep Current Item and set the field to 'Name'.

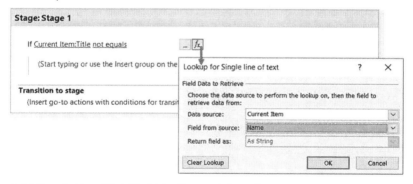

4. Add the Action 'Set Field in Current Item':

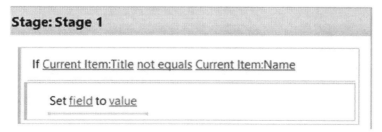

    a. Click on <u>field</u> and select 'Title' from the dropdown.

95

b. Click on <u>value</u> and open the Function Builder.

c. Keep Current Item and set the field to 'Name'.

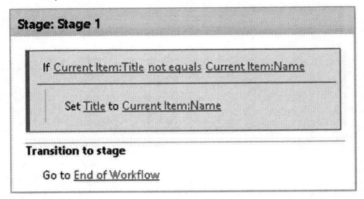

5. Set the workflow to start automatically when an item is created (or changed, *refer* to the Theory section above).

6. Check, publish and test the workflow.

Demo:

http://kalmstrom.com/Tips/SharePoint-Workflows/Title-List-Workflow.htm

17.4 REUSABLE WORKFLOW TO SET TITLE

I imagine that you want to use a workflow like this one on multiple document libraries, and if that is true, I recommend you to instead create a reusable workflow connected to the document library content type.

17.4.1 Theory: Reusable Workflow

If you want to be able to use the workflow again, you should create a reusable workflow. Reusable workflows can be saved as workflow templates, and these can be connected to multiple lists or libraries. Reusable workflows are most often associated with a specific content type, and the testing is not done until after that association.

For reusable workflows, the start options are set in the site collection where the workflow will be used. In *SharePoint Designer*, the reusable workflows can only be disabled.

17.4.1.1 Connect the Reusable Workflow to a Content Type

Reusable workflows are most often assigned to a specific content type. In those cases, it must be a SharePoint 2010 workflow, because SharePoint 2013 workflows cannot be connected to a specific content type.

When you create a reusable workflow and connect it to a content type, the workflow will be used in all apps in the site collection that have that content type.

When you assign the reusable workflow to a content type, you must do it twice. First you must assign it in *SharePoint Designer*, when you create the workflow. This gives the workflow access to the columns of the content type.

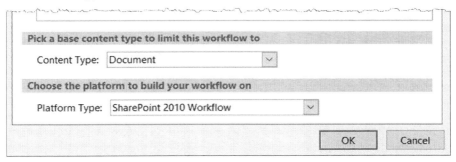

You must also assign content type in the site collection(s) where you want to use the workflow. When you do that in the root site of the site collection, the workflow will be applied in all apps that are based on the associated content type in that site collection:

1. Open the Site settings in the root site of the site collection and click on the 'Site content types' link in the Web Designer Galleries group.

   Web Designer Galleries
   Site columns
   Site content types

2. Select the Content Types group, and then click on the content type you want to use the workflow with.

97

3. Click on the Workflow settings link.

4. Click on Add a workflow. Now you will follow steps similar to when you added a built-in workflow to a list in chapter 3.

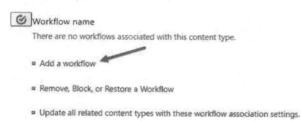

5. Select a workflow template. (You might have to activate it. In that case there is an Activate button.)

6. Give the workflow a name. You can also give specific names to the workflow's tasks and history lists.

7. Set the workflow to start when an item is created or changed, if that is what you need. Decide if the default Edit permission is enough to start the workflow, or if you should require Manage Lists permission. (You can also leave the start options blank, in case you want to start the workflow with a timer; *refer to* 19.5.1, Theory: Retention Stage.)

Start Options

Specify how this workflow can be
started.

☑ Allow this workflow to be manually started by an authenticated user with Edit Item permissions.

☐ Require Manage Lists Permissions to start the workflow.

☐ Creating a new item will start this workflow.

☐ Changing an item will start this workflow.

Update List and Site Content
Types

Update all related content types
with these settings? It may take a
while.

Add this workflow to all related content types?

◉ Yes   ○ No

8. Make sure that you select 'Yes' for 'Add this workflow to all content types that inherit from this content type?' or 'Add this workflow to all related content types?', before you click OK.

Now all the site collection's existing and new libraries that use the content type will have this workflow.

(If you only want to assign the workflow to one list, you can open the list settings and then the Workflow Settings for that list. Click on 'Add a workflow' and select the content type and then the workflow you want to add.)

17.4.2 Steps

To connect the reusable workflow with the Document content type, you must create a SharePoint 2010 workflow, because SharePoint 2013 workflows cannot be connected to a specific content type.

The condition and action are set just like in the list workflow above.

1. Click on 'Workflows' in the *SharePoint Designer* left pane.

1. Click on the Reusable Workflow button in the ribbon.

2. Give the workflow a name and select the workflow type SharePoint 2010. Assign the workflow to the Document content type.

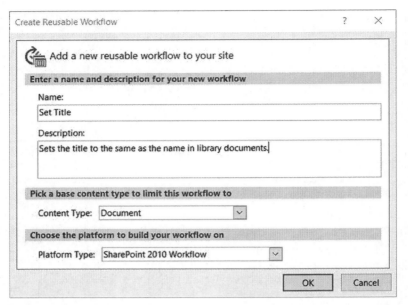

3. Select the Condition to 'If current item field equals value' and set it to 'Title' 'not equals' 'Name'.

4. Select the Action 'Set Field in Current Item' and set the Field to 'Title' and the Value to 'Name'.

5. Do *not* set any start options. That will be done when you associate the workflow with the content type.

6. Check and publish the workflow.

7. Associate the workflow with the 'Document' content type:

    a. In the root site of the site collection, open the Site settings >Site content types.

    b. Show the group Document Content Types.

    c. Click on the 'Document' content type.

    Document Content Types

    Basic Page

    Document

    a. Open the workflow settings and click on 'Add a workflow'.

    b. Select the reusable workflow you just created.

    c. Give the workflow a name.

d. Set the workflow to start automatically when an item is created (or changed).

Now this workflow will be used in all lists that use the Document content type in that site collection. To use the workflow in other site collections, *refer to* 18.4.1, Theory: Save a Reusable Workflow as a Template.

Demo:

http://kalmstrom.com/Tips/SharePoint-Workflows/Title-Reusable-Workflow.htm

18 PHONE MESSAGE ALERT WORKFLOWS

In this chapter I will show a workflow for e-mail alerts about missed telephone calls. We imagine a company where reception staff answers incoming calls. If the person who was called was not available, the receptionist who took the call adds info about the call in a SharePoint list.

The alert message contains the name and telephone number of the person who called and info about who received the call. There is also a link to the list item in edit mode, so that the called person quickly can mark the call as returned.

We will create this workflow both as a list workflow and as a reusable workflow, just like in the previous chapter. For this reusable workflow, we will also create a template, so that it can be used in other site collections.

18.1 PREREQUISITES

A custom SharePoint list, *Phone Messages*. The 'Title' column is renamed to "Caller phone number". There are also three other columns, all mandatory:

- A Single line of text column, "Caller name".
- A Person or Group column, "Called", for the person who was called.
- A Yes/No column, "Returned", where the default value is No.

For the reusable workflow, these columns are site columns in the content type "Phone Message". For the list workflow, the columns can be list columns.

18.2 THEORY: DATE/TIME FORMAT

In this workflow, we will create a lookup with a date/time return field when we add the dynamic content for 'Created' in the e-mail body. *SharePoint Designer* gives many options on how to format the date and time in the dropdown 'Return field as'. All those dates formats rely on the regional settings of the site in which the workflow runs.

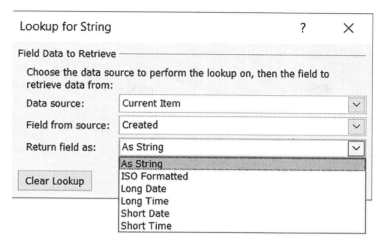

These are the outcomes:

- As String: 17/8/2018 12.05.00 AM
- ISO Formatted: 2018-08-17T12.05.00Z
- Long Date: Friday, August 17, 2018
- Long Time: 12.05.00 AM
- Short Date: 17/8 2018
- Short Time: 12:05 AM

18.3 LIST WORKFLOW

This workflow sends an e-mail to the person who was called when someone adds a new item with information about that call in the *Phone Messages* list. The e-mail body has caller information and a link to the list item, so that the call smoothly can be set to Returned.

1. Create a list workflow for the *Phone Messages* list.

2. Go to the end of the workflow.

3. Add the Action 'Send an Email'.

    a. Click on <u>these users</u>.

    b. At 'To', open the Function Builder.

        i. Select 'Workflow Lookup for a User' and click on 'Add'.

        ii. Keep Current Item and select 'Called' and 'Email Address'.

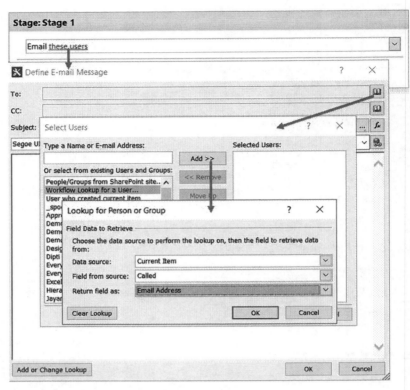

c. For the subject, open the String Builder.

    i.   Enter hard-coded text, "Phone call from".

    ii.   Click on 'Add or Change Lookup'.

    iii.   Keep Current Item and select 'Caller name'.

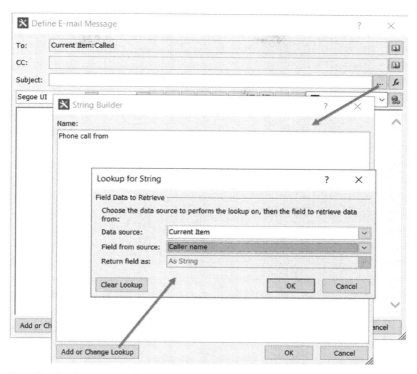

d. For the body, open the String Builder and add hard-coded text and lookups on three rows, for the Current Item phone number, created time and creator and a link to the current item in edit mode:

    i.   Hard-code "The phone number is:"

    ii.   Click on 'Add or Change Lookup' and select 'Caller phone number'.

    iii.   Hard-code "The call was received at:"

    iv.   Click on 'Add or Change Lookup' and select 'Created'. Also select your preferred time format.

    v.   After the 'Created' lookup, continue by writing "by" and adding a lookup for 'Created by'.

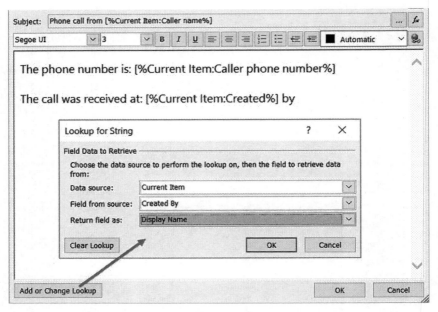

vi. Hard-code "Set the call to Returned".

vii. Select the text and click on the hyperlink icon. Now the text you wrote will be visible as anchor text.

viii. Open the String Builder at the Address field.

ix. Add the link to the item in edit form as described above in 14.3.1 Theory: Link to Item in Edit Mode.

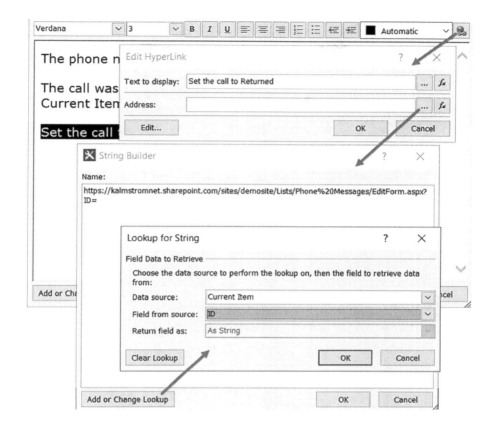

4. Set the workflow to start automatically when an item is created.

5. Check, publish and test the workflow.

The workflow described above is suitable for a simple SharePoint list for phone messages. If you have more advanced phone messages lists connected to a specific content type, I instead suggest a reusable workflow described below.

Demo:

http://www.kalmstrom.com/Tips/SharePoint-Workflows/Phone-Messages-Workflow.htm

https://kalmstrom.com/Tips/SharePoint-Workflows/Phone-Messages-Workflow-Link.htm

18.4 REUSABLE WORKFLOW

When you create a reusable SharePoint 2010 workflow and connect the workflow to a content type, it can be used in all lists in the site collection that have this content type. Note that it must be a 2010 workflow. SharePoint 2013 workflows can only be connected to all content types.

18.4.1 Theory: Save a Reusable Workflow as a Template

When you have published a reusable workflow, you can save it as a template. It will then be saved as a WSP file in the Site Assets library of the site where you created the workflow.

1. In *SharePoint Designer*, open the settings for the reusable workflow and click on the 'Save as Template' button in the ribbon. (The 'Publish Globally' button that is greyed out in the image below, only publishes the workflow within the site collection.)

2. Download the WSP file from the Site Assets library to your PC and then upload it to other site collections to use it there.

3. Open the Site settings in the root site of the site collection where you want to use the workflow.

4. Click on 'Solutions' in the Web Designer Galleries group.

5. Upload the WSP file and activate it to make it available for the whole site collection.

6. Open the site settings again and click on the 'Manage site features' link in the Site Actions group, to activate the workflow for the site.

7. Find the reusable workflow in the list and activate it. (Note that you must activate twice, first under 'Solutions' and then under 'Manage site features', even if you are using the template in the root site of the site collection.)

8. When the activation has finished, you will see an Active icon, and the Activate button has been replaced by a Deactivate button.

9. Connect the workflow to a content type for the site collection as described in 17.4.1.1 above.

18.4.2 Steps

For the reusable workflow, we can use the same actions and lookups as in the 2013 list workflow above. The start options are however not set in the reusable workflow. Instead it is set each time you associate the workflow with a list.

1. Create a reusable workflow and connect it to your "Phone Message" content type.

2. Select the SharePoint 2010 platform.

3. Add the Action 'Send an Email'.

4. Follow the same steps to customize the e-mail as in the list workflow above.

5. Check and publish the workflow.

6. Associate the workflow with the "Phone Message" content type, for use in the current site collection, *refer to* 17.4.1.1, Connect the Reusable Workflow to a Content Type.

7. Save the workflow as a template.

8. Download the WSP file from the Site Assets library and then upload it to the site collection where you also want to use it.

9. Activate the WSP file for the site collection and for the site.

10. Associate the workflow with the content type in the new site collection.

11. (Activate the workflow in more sites in the site collection and/or upload it to more site collections and repeat the process.)

Demo:

https://www.kalmstrom.com/Tips/SharePoint-Workflows/Phone-Messages-Enterprise-Reusable-Workflow.htm

19 RENTAL AGREEMENT RENEWALS

In this rather long chapter, we will create two example workflows. Both are intended for rental agreements. The workflows are connected so that the first one sets a date and the other one sends a reminder on that date:

- A workflow that sets the renewal date of rental agreements to two months before the end date of the agreement, if no other date is specified in a "Renewal Date" column. This can be a SharePoint 2010 or SharePoint 2013 workflow.

- A workflow that sends a reminder e-mail to the person who is responsible for the rental agreements. This must be a SharePoint 2010 workflow.

19.1 PREREQUISITES

A custom *Rental Agreements* list where the Title column is renamed to "Location". The list also has the following list or site columns:

- A Date and Time column, "End Date".

- A Date and Time column, "Renewal Date".

- A Person or Group column, "Responsible".

19.2 THEORY: LOCAL VARIABLE

In this and several of the following workflow examples we will use a local variable. A variable can be selected in a Lookup dialog whenever you need the variable value in the workflow.

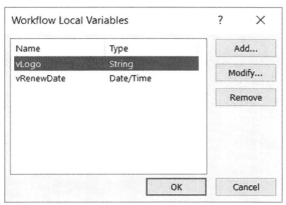

To manage local variables, click on the 'Local Variable' button in the *SharePoint Designer ribbon*. In the dialog that opens, you can Add, Modify and Remove variables.

Name	Type	
vLogo	String	Add...
vRenewDate	Date/Time	Modify...
		Remove

Workflow Local Variables ? ✕

OK   Cancel

19.2.1 Create a New Local Variable

To create a new Local Variable, click on the 'Local Variable' button in the ribbon to open the 'Workflow Local Variables' dialog, *see* above. Then click on 'Add':

1. Give the variable a name. It is suitable to use CamelCase naming, and I sometimes add a "v" before the name to indicate that it is a variable.

2. Select Type.

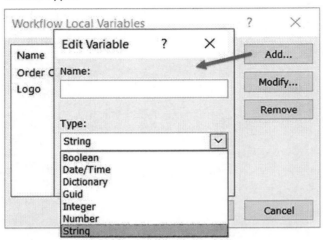

19.2.2 Set Variable Value

Local variables must not have a value that is longer than 255 characters. If the value is longer, break the variable in two and use both.

The value of a variable can be set in two ways.

*   Use the action 'Set Workflow Variable' when you want the variable to have an already existing value:

    Set <u>workflow variable</u> to <u>value</u>

*   Click on <u>workflow variable</u> and select one of your variables. (You can also create a new variable from here.)

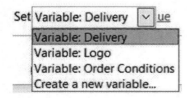

- Then click on value and write in text or open the String or Function Builder to continue building the variable with a string or a lookup.

Set Variable: Delivery to |

- Use the action 'Do Calculation' when you want to give the variable a calculated value.

Calculate value plus value (Output to Variable: calc)

a. Click on the two value links and select which parameters should be used in the calculation.

b. Click on 'plus' to set the calculation mode. ('mod' returns the remainder after a number is divided by a divisor.)

plus ⌄
plus
minus
multiply by
divided by
mod

c. For the output you can either use the default 'Variable: calc' or click on the link to create a new variable.

To see example workflows that use variables, *refer to*:

Chapter 22, Progress Bar (calculated value)

Chapter 23, Format E-mail Body (existing value)

19.3 LIST WORKFLOW THAT SETS A DATE

Use a list workflow if the organization only has a few rental agreements, stored in one SharePoint list.

19.3.1 Theory: Column Null value

All SharePoint columns have a "null" value from start, before another value has been added. This is something we can take advantage of to decide if a column is empty or not.

This first example workflow will only run if the "Renewal Date" column is empty. We check if it is with a condition: if the value of the "Renewal Date" column is less than 1970. This is a random value, and any value that is not likely to happen can be used. The point is that a "null" value will be less than the random value. Only then, the workflow action will take place.

19.3.2 Steps

This workflow first checks if the "Renewal Date" column is empty. If it is empty, the workflow sets the renewal date of each new or changed rental agreement to two months before the agreement's end date.

1. Create a SharePoint 2013 or 2010 workflow for the "Rental Agreements" list. (Go to the end of the workflow if you use a 2013 workflow.)

2. Add the Condition 'If current item field equals value':

   a. Click on <u>field</u> and select "Renewal Date".

   b. Click on <u>equals</u> and select 'is less than'.

   c. Click on 'value' and then on the ellipsis. Select 'Specific date' and change the year to 1970.

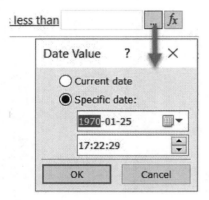

3. Add the Action 'Add Time to Date':

   a. Click on <u>0</u> and write in -2.

   b. Click on <u>minutes</u> and select 'months'.

   c. Click on <u>date</u> and open the Function Builder. Keep Current Item and select 'End Date'.

   d. Click on <u>Variable:date</u> and select to create a new variable. Give it the name vRenewDate and keep the suggested type, Date/Time.

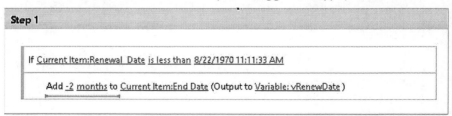

4. Add the Action 'Update List Item':

a. Click on this list

b. Keep Current Item and click on 'Add'.

c. Set the field to 'Renewal Date'.

d. Open the Function Builder to set a value.

e. Select the data source 'Workflow Variables and Parameters'.

f. Select the new variable, 'vRenewDate'.

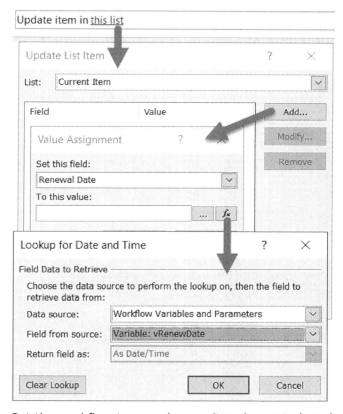

5. Set the workflow to run when an item is created or changed.

6. Check, publish and test the workflow.

19.4 REUSABLE WORKFLOW THAT SETS A DATE

When the organization has more than 5000 rental agreements, they should be stored in multiple SharePoint lists and a specific "Rental Agreement" content type should be created. How to do that is out of scope for this book, but it is described in my book *SharePoint Online from Scratch* and the demos I refer to below are created for that book.

19.4.1 Steps

Step 2-4 are the same as in the list workflow described above.

1. Create a SharePoint 2010 workflow and connect it to the "Rental Agreement" content type.

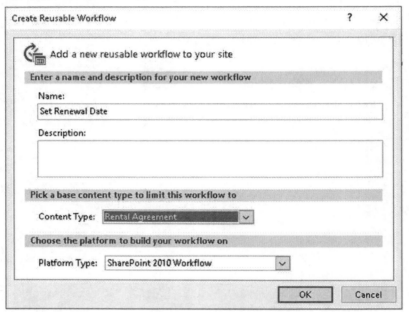

2. Add the Condition 'If current item field equals value'.

3. Add the Action 'Add Time to Date'.

4. Add the Action 'Update List Item'.

5. Check, publish and test the workflow.

6. Associate the Reusable Workflow with the Rental Agreement content type, *refer to* 17.4.1.1, Connect the Reusable Workflow to a Content Type

7. If you want to use the workflow in several site collections, save it as a template. *Refer to* 18.4.1 Theory: Save a Reusable Workflow as a Template.

Demo:

http://www.kalmstrom.com/Tips/SharePoint-Workflows/Rental-Agreements-Reusable-Workflow-Date.htm

19.5 E-MAIL ON RENTAL AGREEMENT RENEWAL

In the sections above, we created a list workflow and a reusable workflow that set the rental agreement renewal date to two months before the end date of the agreement, if the "Renewal Date" column was empty.

On the renewal day, the responsible person should have an e-mail alert about the renewal, whether it was set manually or by a workflow. Here we will create a workflow that sends such a renewal reminder.

19.5.1 Theory: Retention Stage

The second workflow in this chapter, that sends an e-mail, can be either a list workflow or a reusable workflow, but it must be a SharePoint 2010 workflow. The date for the workflow to run and the e-mail to be sent is set by a retention stage either just in the list where you want the workflow to run or in the content type settings. This cannot be done with a SharePoint 2013 workflow.

Start creating the workflow as usual in *SharePoint Designer*. When the workflow has been created, add a retention stage under 'Information management policy settings'.

List:

1. Open the List settings and click on the link 'Information management policy settings'.

2. Click on the link to the content type of the list where you want the workflow to run.

Content type:

1. Open the Site Settings from the root site of the site collection where you want to use the workflow.

2. Click on the 'Site content types' link in the Web Designer Galleries group.

3. Select the content type group that contains the content type and then the content type itself.

4. Click on the 'Information management policy settings' link.

In both cases, enable retention and click on 'Add a retention stage...'.

☑ Enable Retention

Non-Records

Specify how to manage retention on items that have not been declared records:

Items will not expire until a stage is added.

Add a retention stage...

Now you can set your preferences in the dialog that opens. Specify a time and select the action to be 'Run a workflow'. That will give you a selection of your 2010 workflows, so that you can decide which one should be run.

(Retention stages can be used for other actions as well, not just to start a workflow.)

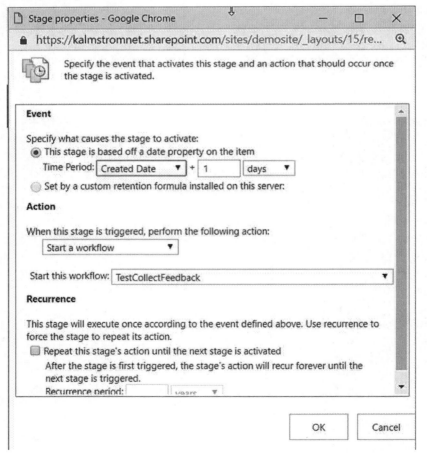

19.5.2 Steps

This workflow can be created as a list workflow or as a reusable workflow. Here I will describe the steps for the list workflow, but by now you hopefully understand the differences and can create a reusable workflow for the e-mail generating instead, if that is what you need.

1. Create a SharePoint 2010 workflow for the "Rental Agreements" list.

2. Add the Action 'Send an Email':

   a. Click on <u>these users</u>.

   b. For the e-mail 'To' field, click on the Lookup icon and select 'Workflow Lookup for a User' and click on 'Add'.

   c. Keep Current Item and select 'Responsible' and 'Email Address'.

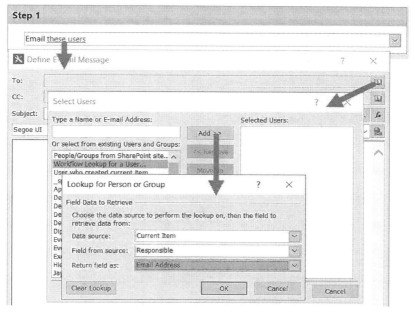

   d. For the e-mail 'Subject' field, open the String Builder and write in "Time to renew the contract for". Add a lookup for the 'Location' value in the Current Item.

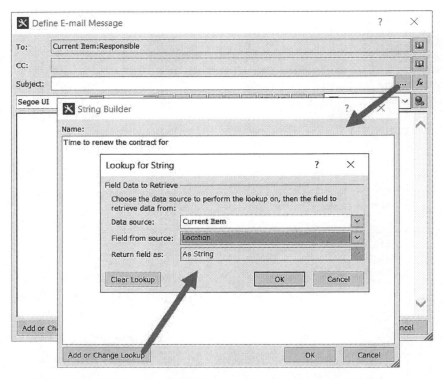

e. Add a link to the rental agreement item in the e-mail body:

    i. Click on the hyperlink icon.

    ii. Add anchor text: "See the agreement".

    iii. At Address, open the Function Builder.

    iv. Select 'Workflow Context' >'Current Item URL'.

3. Open the "Rental Agreements" List settings.

4. Click on the 'Information management policy settings' link and then on the 'Item' content type used in the list.

5. Enable retention and click on 'Add retention stage...':

a. Set the Time Period to the 'Renewal Date' + 0 days.

b. Set the Action to start the workflow that sends the renewal alert.

c. Remember to click OK both to the Retention dialog and to the 'Edit Policy' page!

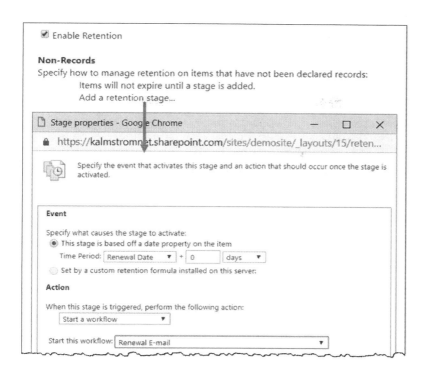

This retention setting cannot be checked immediately, as it is time dependent, but you can make sure that it is active in the Information management policy settings. At the content type, you can see that a Retention Policy has been defined.

Retention Policy Defined

Yes ⟵

When you click on the content type, you can see the retention stage.

Demos:

http://www.kalmstrom.com/Tips/SharePoint-Workflows/Rental-Agreements-Reusable-Workflow-Email.htm

http://www.kalmstrom.com/Tips/SharePoint-Workflows/Rental-Agreements-Timer-Retention.htm

20 CALCULATE TOTALS

The 'Totals' feature can be used to summarize values in a SharePoint column, and the result of the calculation is shown on top of the column that is calculated. In the image below, the sums of hardware and setup costs have been calculated.

It is however *not* possible to use Totals for a column with calculated values, like the "Total Cost" column in the image, where the values have been calculated from the hardware and setup costs. I have pointed to the issue with a red line where the sum should have been.

⊕ **new item** or edit this list

	All Items ⋯	Find an item 🔍			
✓	Title		Hardware Cost	Setup Cost	Total Cost
			Sum= $1,700	**Sum= $350**	▬▬▬▬
	Kalle's laptop ✳	⋯	$500	$100	$600
	Stina's tablet ✳	⋯	$400	$50	$450
	Bert's desktop ✳	⋯	$800	$200	$1,000

To solve the problem, we can let a workflow do the calculation and update the column. Then the "row sum" can have calculated values and the SharePoint 'Totals' feature can be used on the column.

This example workflow calculates the sum of values in two currency columns and updates a third currency column with that sum. As we use a currency column for the result of the calculation – and not a calculated column – we can use the Totals feature without problems and see the Totals for the workflow calculated column.

⊕ **new item** or edit this list

	All Items ⋯	Find an item 🔍			
✓	Title		Hardware Cost	Setup Cost	Total Cost
			Sum= $2,000	**Sum= $550**	**Sum= $2,550**
	Kalle's laptop ✳	⋯	$500	$100	$600
	Stina's tablet ✳	⋯	$400	$50	$450
	Bert's desktop ✳	⋯	$800	$200	$1,000

Unfortunately, the Totals feature can only be used in lists with the classic interface when this is written, but it will hopefully soon be added to modern lists too.

20.1 PREREQUISITES:

A SharePoint *Computers* list with the classic interface and three currency columns: "Hardware Cost", "Setup Cost" and "Total Cost". (The internal names are in CamelCase writing.)

The view should be modified so that all three columns use the Total Sum feature.

The values in the "Total Cost" column will be calculated by the workflow.

20.2 THEORY: CALCULATION VARIABLE

In this example we will update a list item's "Total Cost" column each time an item is created or changed, but that cannot be done with a calculation directly in an action. Instead, we will create a local variable that gets its value from a 'Do Calculation' action, *refer to* 19.2, Theory: Local Variable. This variable will then be used in a 'Set Field in Current Item' action.

Here we will create a new local variable for the calculation value. It is of course possible to just keep the automatically created variable "calc", but I prefer to create a new variable with a more descriptive name and remove the "calc" variable.

Local variables have no "currency" type, so we will use the type 'Number' for the output variable.

20.3 STEPS

This workflow first calculates the sum of the current item values in the "Setup Cost" and "Hardware Cost" columns. After that, it sets the current item value in the "Total Cost" column to the result of that calculation.

1. Create a blank flow and use the trigger 'SharePoint – When an item is created or modified' for the *Computers* list.

2. Go to the end of the workflow.

3. Add the action 'Do Calculation'.

   Calculate value plus value (Output to Variable: calc)

   a. Click on the first value and open the Function Builder.

b. Set the value to be the 'Setup Cost' of the Current Item. (The return value from reading a currency column is automatically set to 'As Double', because that is how SharePoint stores the currency numbers internally.)

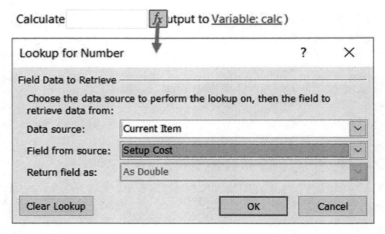

c. Keep 'plus'.

d. Click on the second <u>value</u> and open the Function Builder.

e. Set the value to be the 'Hardware Cost' of the Current Item.

f. Click on 'Variable calc' and select to create a new variable. Give the new variable the name "vTotalCalculatedCost" and keep the type 'Number'.

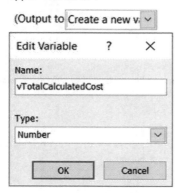

g. Now the 'Do Calculation' action will look like this:

Calculate <u>Current Item:Setup Cost</u> <u>plus</u> <u>Current Item:Hardware Cost</u> (Output to <u>Variable: vTotalCalculatedCost</u>)

4. Add the action 'Set Field in Current Item'.

a. Click on 'field' and select 'Total Cost' from the dropdown.

b. Click on <u>value</u> and open the Function Builder.

c. Select the new variable from the Data source 'Workflow Variables and Parameters'.

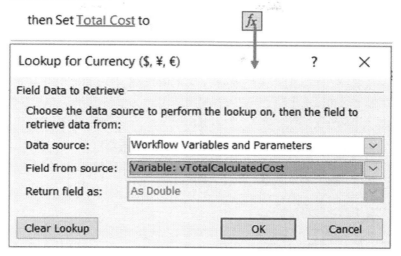

5. Click on the 'Local Variable' button in the ribbon and remove the 'calc' variable from the workflow.

6. Set the workflow to start automatically when an item is created or changed.

7. Check, publish and test the workflow.

Demo:

https://www.kalmstrom.com/Tips/SharePoint-Workflows/Totals-Workflow.htm

21 SITE WORKFLOWS WITH INITIATION FORM

In this chapter we will create two example flows where we use a site workflow and an initiation form. We will use this combination to create a one field form for e-mail sending and to give a simple version of a more complicated SharePoint form.

21.1 THEORY: INITIATION FORM AND SITE WORKFLOW

Site workflows and initiation forms are often used together, but that is not necessary. Other workflows can also use an initiation form, and site workflows can be used for other purposes.

21.1.1 Initiation Form

An initiation form is a SharePoint page that opens each time a workflow is started. In *SharePoint Designer* such initiation forms are built with the 'Initiation Form Parameters' command.

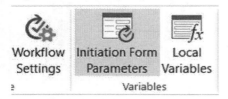

When you click on the 'Initiation Form Parameters' button, a dialog will open where you can add your required parameters. These parameters will show up as fields in a form.

Add a field name and a description and select column type. When you click on 'Next' you can add a default value for the field. There might also be some other settings, depending on which type of information the column contains.

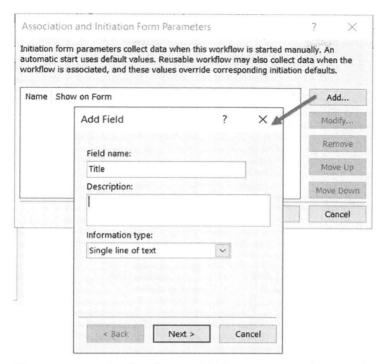

When a parameter has been added, we can use them in the workflow each time we need the value of that parameter.

21.1.2 Site Workflow

A site workflow is not connected to a list or library but runs on site level. It can for example track events in a site and run reports on them or send e-mails to a group of people. Site workflows are started from another workflow or from a hyperlink.

To create a site workflow, click on the 'Site Workflow' button. The creation dialog looks like the list workflow dialog.

You can let a list workflow start a site workflow that is built on the SharePoint 2010 platform.

Another option is to start the workflow manually, and in that case, it can be built on both SharePoint platforms. In the Site contents, click on 'Site workflows' and then on the workflow you want to start. It is also here you can see the status of the site workflow.

21.2 Send Standard E-Mail

The first workflow that uses an initiation form is very simple, just to show the idea. It sends an e-mail to people that can be different for each sending. The content of the e-mail is however the same each time.

This example site workflow is started manually at times when the e-mail needs to be sent. The workflow sends the same e-mail each time, but the recipients are entered in the initiation form for each sending occasion.

Here we imagine a manager that sometimes need to remind staff about a requested report, but the same kind of workflow can be used for any e-mail that has standard text in the e-mail body. The text can of course have dynamic content so that it still becomes different each time.

Start: Send Report Reminder

Report Reminder Recipients

Peter Kalmström x |

| Start | Cancel |

21.2.1 Prerequisites

A standard e-mail reminder about a report that needs to be sent to a manager.

21.2.2 Steps

In this workflow we first add one initiation form parameter for e-mail recipients. Then we add an action that sends an e-mail to the recipients that are added in the form each time the workflow is run.

1. Create a site workflow.

2. Go to the end of the workflow.

3. Add an initiation form parameter:

   a. Click on 'Add' and write in the Field name "Report reminder recipients".

   b. At 'Information type' select 'Person or Group'.

   c. Click on 'Next' and check the box for multiple values.

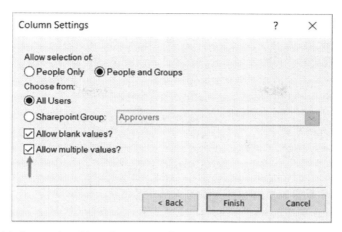

4. Add the action 'Send an Email':

   a. At 'To' open the Function Builder and select 'Workflow Lookup for a User…'. Click on 'Add'.

   b. Select the data source 'Workflow Variables and Parameters' and then the new initiation parameter you created in the step above. Set the return field to 'Email Addresses, Semicolon Delimited'.

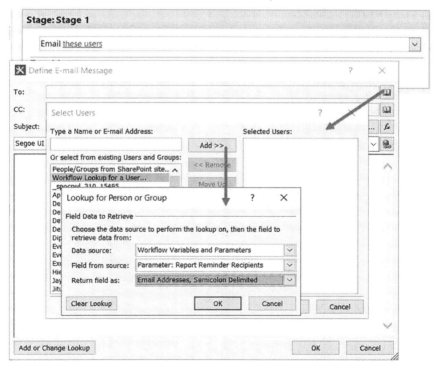

5. Publish the workflow.

6. To test, open Site Contents >Site workflows in SharePoint and click on the new workflow. Send an e-mail to yourself.

21.3 FORM THAT FEEDS TO TASKS ITEM

Helpdesk and support staff often use SharePoint lists to manage reported issues. In some organizations the end users are asked to create new items in that list as a way of reporting problems, but that is not an optimal process. For proper issue tracking, the helpdesk staff needs to have more information in each item than what is given by the person who has the problem.

A better solution is to give the end users a simple form that is easy to reach and fill out. A workflow can copy the data entered there into the more detailed form used by the helpdesk people.

With such a workflow, end users never have to see a detailed task form. Instead they can just click on a workflow link or button and fill out the simple form.

21.3.1 Prerequisites

A SharePoint "Tasks" list built on the tasks or issue tracking template.

21.3.2 Theory: Start Link in the Quick Launch

This workflow is started manually and opens a simple form, where the person who wants to report a problem can enter a title and a description. The workflow then copies that information to a new item in a SharePoint tasks list, where the support staff can take care of it and fill out the rest of the fields.

A link at Site contents >Site workflows opens the form and starts the workflow. For users it is however more convenient to have the link in the Quick Launch, where they can reach it more easily:

1. In the SharePoint site where you created the site workflow, open Site contents >Site workflows.

2. Right-click on the workflow link and select 'Copy link address'.

3. Edit the Quick Launch on the homepage and add the link you copied.

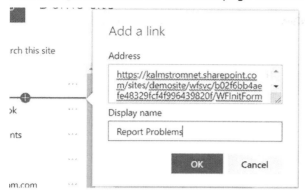

21.3.3 *Steps*

In this example workflow, we first set the two initiation form parameters and then add an action to create a list item in a SharePoint tasks list. This action feeds the text entered by the end users in the initiation form to the corresponding fields in the tasks list.

1. Open the site that has the "Tasks" list in SharePoint Designer and create a site workflow.

2. Go to the end of the workflow.

3. Click on the 'Initiation Form Parameters' button and add two parameters. Leave the default value blank for both.

    a. Title, Single line of text.

    b. Description, multiple lines of text.

4. Add the action 'Create List Item':

    a. Click on this list.

    b. Select the "Tasks" list.

    c. Select 'Title' and click on 'Modify'.

    d. Open the Function Builder.

    e. Select 'Workflow Variables and Parameters' and 'Parameter: Title'.

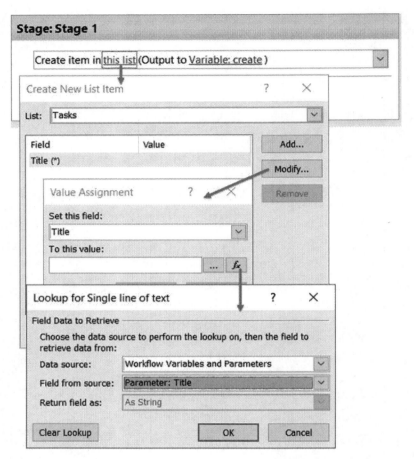

f. Click OK to everything except the first 'Create New List Item' dialog.

g. Click on 'Add' and Select the 'Description' field.

h. Open the Function Builder.

i. Select 'Workflow Variables and Parameters' and 'Parameter: Description'.

j. Check, publish and test the workflow.

(When the workflow works as it should, add a start link in the Quick Launch.)

Demo:

https://www.kalmstrom.com/Tips/SharePoint-Workflows/Initiation-Forms.htm

22 PROGRESS BAR

This example workflow will add a progress bar to a *Tickets* list. It reads the value in the "% Complete" column and makes a graphic representation of that value in a separate column.

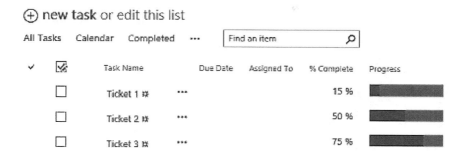

The technique I show here can be used whenever you want to add dynamic HTML code to a SharePoint list column, for example for conditional formatting.

22.1 PREREQUISITES:

- A SharePoint *Tickets* list built on the Tasks template. It has a custom multiple lines of text column called "Progress".

  The "Progress" column is added to the default view, and the default formatting option for this column, 'Enhanced rich text', is kept.

- A piece of HTML code for the progress bar. Here we use HTML code for a table with one row and two columns. The right column needs to have a min-height value, so that it is visible even if it has no content.

  The code used in the image above is:

  `<table style="width: 100px; border: 0px">,`

  `<tr>`

  `<td style="padding: 0px; width: `**`100`**`px; background-color: green"></td>`

  `<td style="padding: 0px; min-height: 16px; background-color: red"></td>`

  `</tr>`

  `</table>`

  Note: "100" is bold above, because in the workflow it will be replaced by a lookup for a variable that calculates the required width.

22.2 THEORY: PERCENT CALCULATION

The SharePoint Tasks template gives a list that has a checkbox and a "% Complete" column with the default value of 0. When the box is checked, the value of the % Complete column will change to 100. Other values are set manually in the item form.

In this example flow, we will calculate the percentage of the value of each item's "% Complete" column and output the result to a custom variable.

The "% Complete" value is stored in SharePoint as a % number, – a decimal between 0 (0%) and 1 (100%) – so you can create such a function by multiplying the value of the column that should be calculated with 100.

Example: a task that is halfway done would appear as 50%. For it to display as 50 pixels wide (half of the 100 pixels the progress bar is), we multiply the 0,5 by 100.

22.3 STEPS

The workflow is triggered when an item is created or changed. It reads the value in the "% Complete" column and sets the width of the left column according to that value. The right column will be adjusted automatically, as the table has a fixed width of 100 pixels.

1. Create a list workflow for the *Tickets* list.

2. Go to the end of the workflow.

3. Create a Local Variable called "Percent". The Type should be 'Number'.

4. Add the action 'Do Calculation' to give the variable a value.

   a. Click on the first <u>value</u> and open the Function Builder.

   b. Keep 'Current Item' and select the '% Completed' field.

   c. Click on 'plus' and select 'multiply by'.

   d. Click on the second <u>value</u> and write in '100'.

   e. Click on 'Variable:calc' and set the output to the "Percent" variable that you created in step 3.

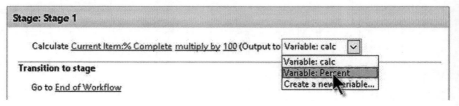

5. Add an 'Update List Item' action for the "Progress" column.

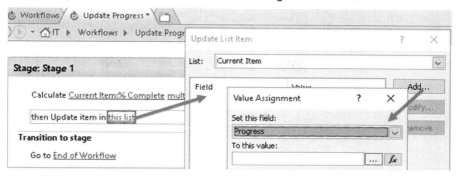

a. Click on 'this list'.

b. Keep 'Current Item' and click on 'Add'.

c. Select the "Progress" column.

d. Open the String Builder and paste the HTML code.

e. Select "100" and replace it with a lookup for the Percent variable.

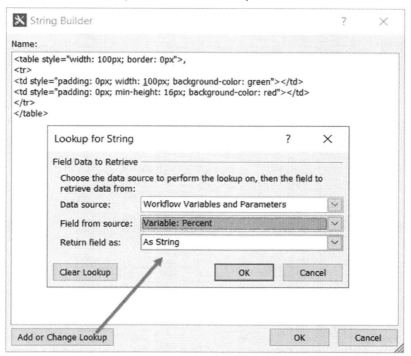

f. Now the HTML in the String Builder looks like this:

```
<table style="width: 100px; border: 0px">,
<tr>
<td style="padding: 0px; width: [%Variable: Percent%]px; background-color: green"></td>
<td style="padding: 0px; min-height: 16px; background-color: red"></td>
</tr>
</table>
```

6. Set the workflow to start automatically when an item is created or changed.

7. Check, publish and test the workflow.

Demo:

https://kalmstrom.com/Tips/SharePoint-Workflows/Progress-Bar-Workflow.htm

23 FORMAT E-MAIL BODY

In this example we will add a table to the body of a workflow generated e-mail that is sent when a new item is added to a SharePoint list. Here I have chosen to use a file and a SharePoint *Procedures* document library as an example.

The reason for the e-mail can be just information, or it can be an approval e-mail, but for this example the reason does not matter. Here we will just create an e-mail with a table and an image in the body.

In each e-mail, the table is filled out with dynamic content for the file name and the creator of the new file.

I also describe how to add an image to the e-mail body by using a local variable.

23.1 PREREQUISITES:

A SharePoint document library, *Procedures*.

A table created in Word.

An image tag. I recommend that you use an image that is placed within your own farm/tenant. If you use an image from outside, the receiver of the e-mail might need to allow the image download.

Here is an example piece of code, that gives the *SharePoint Designer* icon:

```
<img
src="http://www.kalmstrom.com/images/Microsoft/SharePointDesigner64x64.png
" style="border: 0px; height: 64px; width: 64px" />
```

23.2 THEORY: HTML CODE IN E-MAIL BODY

The *SharePoint Designer* e-mail body has a rich text HTML editor that allows changes in font, style and color, as well as lists or links. Creating more advanced HTML, like tables and images, is not supported.

With the method I describe here, you can however add both tables and images to the body of an automatic e-mail sent by a workflow, or to the description field in a SharePoint list item.

23.2.1 *Images*

A good option for images is to use HTML code by copying image code that has been written in an HTML editor. However, you cannot paste the code directly into the e-mail body field in *SharePoint Designer*. Instead, you should use a local variable, as I describe in the steps below.

23.2.2 *Tables*

For tables, HTML code in a local variable does not work well. Instead, you can create a table in Word and paste it into the e-mail body field in *SharePoint Designer*. The HTML code behind the Word table will automatically be translated into suitable *SharePoint Designer* code when you paste the table.

You can add and change text in the table and add the dynamic content you want to use. You cannot change the table's column with inside *SharePoint Designer*, but the column width will be changed automatically when you add a lookup.

23.2.2.1　E-mail Sender

Workflow generated e-mails cannot always be answered. By default the sender is fetched from the Outgoing Email settings in the Central Administration for SharePoint on-premises. For SharePoint Online, the sender address is no-reply@sharepointonline.com. Therefore, I have set the 'Created by' Return field as 'Email Address' in the table. That way, the receiver can reach the creator of the new procedure.

23.3 STEPS

In this workflow we add HTML code for an image in a local variable that is used in the body of a workflow generated e-mail. In the body we also add a table with dynamic content.

1. Create a list workflow for the *Procedures* library.

2. Go to the end of the workflow.

3. Create a Local Variable for the image and set the value by adding HTML code for an image in the String Builder.

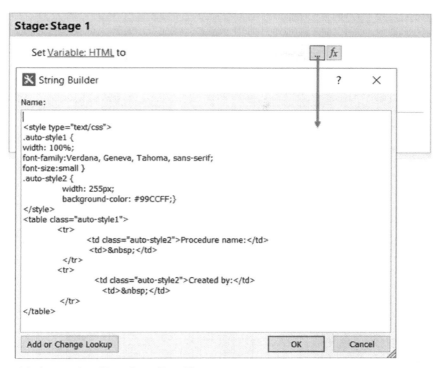

4. Add the Action 'Send an Email':

   a. Add the receiver (or yourself, for testing).

   b. Add a subject.

   c. In the e-mail body, paste a table from Word.

      i. Add a lookup for 'Procedure name'. Set the return field to 'Name'.

      ii. Add a lookup for 'Created by'. Set the Return field to 'Email Address'.

   d. In the e-mail body, under the table, add a lookup for the image variable you created in step 3.

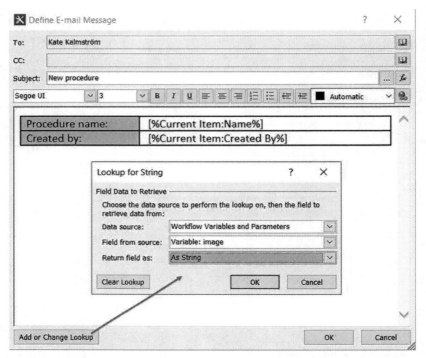

5. Set the workflow to start automatically when an item is created (or changed).

6. Check, publish and test the workflow.

In a more elaborate workflow generated e-mail, there would of course be a link to the new item, but here my purpose is only to show the table and image formatting. For information on how to add a link, *refer to* 15.3.1, Link to Item in Edit Mode.

Demo:

https://www.kalmstrom.com/Tips/SharePoint-Workflows/WF-E-mail-Formatting.htm

24 UNIQUE PERMISSIONS

We will once again look at an example workflow that requires the SharePoint 2010 platform. This time, we will set unique permissions on new files in a SharePoint library, and that cannot be done with a SharePoint 2013 workflow.

For this example workflow, we imagine a teaching situation where files must be submitted to a SharePoint library by the students. Only the teacher should be allowed to see all the files. Each student should only see his/her own file.

24.1 PREREQUISITES

A SharePoint document library, *Homework*.

A possibility to test the workflow as another user than the teacher and the person who created the trigger item.

24.2 THEORY: IMPERSONATION STEP

SharePoint 2010 workflows have a control for an 'Impersonation Step' in the ribbon 'Insert' group.

The Impersonation Step takes the permissions of the last person who published the workflow instead of using the permission of the person who triggered the workflow, which is the normal case (*refer to* 7.4, Workflow Permissions).

By using impersonation, you can let a workflow perform actions that require a higher permission level than what the person who triggers the workflow normally has.

When you add an action or condition to an Impersonation Step, you will have several options connected to permission levels that are not available in other actions and conditions.

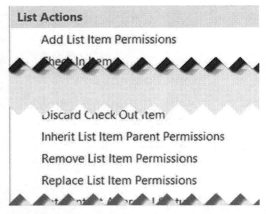

As the Impersonation Step is run as the workflow publisher, you have to consider which account to use in the creation. If that account is blocked or removed, the workflow will stop running. Therefore, it is best to use a service account that never expires for workflows with Impersonation Steps.

The Impersonation Step has to be its own block. If you for example need to use a condition for the impersonation action, you need to put it inside the impersonation step (and not the other way around).

Impersonation Step

The contents of this step will run as the workflow author:

If value equals value

Stop the workflow and log this message

This example workflow uses an Impersonation Step. We let the workflow replace the permissions in the item that triggered the workflow. The permission is set to Full Control for the user who creates the item and for the teacher.

Other users of this list will not have any permissions at all for the item that triggered the workflow – not even read permission. The workflow will remove all inherited or set permissions for the item that triggered the workflow.

It is also possible to select other lists and specify fields for the Impersonation Step.

24.3 STEPS

In this workflow we first add an Impersonation step instead of the first step. We then add a "replace permission" action to the Impersonation step, so that the workflow replaces the inherited permissions for each new library file with Full Control for the teacher and the document creator. By this replacement, other users of the library get no access at all to the new file. The workflow runs each time a new file is created.

1. Create a list workflow on the SharePoint 2010 platform for the *Homework* library.

2. Click on the Step 1 top banner to make the 'Impersonation Step' button in the ribbon active.

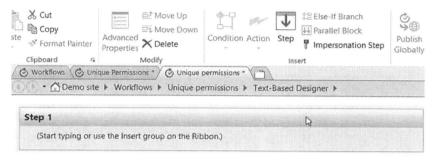

3. Add the Impersonation Step to the workflow.

4. Remove Step 1.

5. Add the action 'Replace List Item Permissions'.

   a. Click on 'these permissions' and then on 'Add' in the dialog that opens.

   b. Check the box for Full Control.

   c. Click on 'Choose...'.

   d. Type or select the people who should have Full Control over the item (the teacher and the user who created the current item). Click on 'Add' between each person.

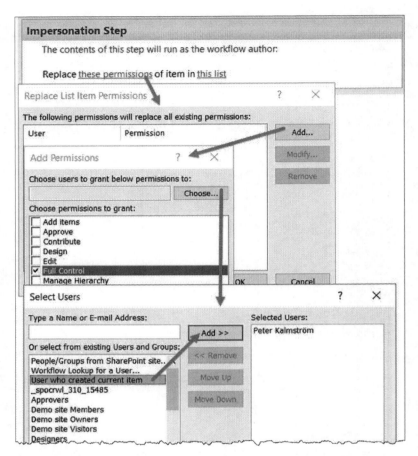

e. Click on 'this list' and then click OK to the default value 'Current item'.

Now the step will look like this. The text "Replace Full Control" is confusing, because it is actually the earlier permissions that have been replaced *with* Full Control.

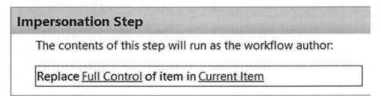

6. Set the workflow to start automatically when an item is created.

7. Check, publish and test the workflow. At publication, you will have a warning about the impersonation permission.

Demo:

https://www.kalmstrom.com/Tips/SharePoint-Workflows/WF-Unique-Permissions.htm

25 MULTIPLE STEPS APPROVALS

Sometimes you need to have documents approved in several steps, one after another, and in this example, we will create a workflow that handles the process.

Note that this is a totally custom solution. It does neither use the built-in 'Approval Status' column nor the built-in Approval workflow that we looked at in 3.4.1, Approval.

The benefit of using a custom approval solution is that it gives you total control of the process. The downside is that the workflow is rather complex and time-consuming to create.

Procedure approvals

Here we imagine an approval process where three teams are involved: Construction, Security and Legal. New procedure documents must be approved by all three teams in that order. If one of the teams reject the document, the workflow will stop running.

In this workflow I focus on the possibility to track what happens with the documents. Security is not first priority, because all steps can be followed by users. The workflow can be disrupted if users change the values in the different "Procedures" columns, but any such manual changes will be visible in the Version History.

The stages in this workflow are visible to all users, so it is important that you give them names that describe what happens in each stage. You can see the names I have used in the first image under Prerequisites. Also *refer to* 8.1.3, Naming.

25.1 PREREQUISITES:

- A "Procedures" document library with
  - A Yes/No choice column for "All Approved", displayed in the default view.
  - Three Yes/No choice columns for the approval decisions, "[TEAM] Approved", not displayed in the default view but used in the workflow.

o Three Person or Group columns for the approvers, "[TEAM] Approved By", not displayed in the default view but used in the workflow.

In the image below, I have called the workflow 'New Procedure Approval', which becomes the name of the status column that is added automatically by the workflow.

Procedures

🗋	Name ∨	All Approved ∨	New Procedure Approval ∨
☒	3TypesOfSiteCollections.xlsx	No	Legal Rejected
🗋	Ana.txt	No	Waiting for Construction Approval
☒	Customers.xlsx	No	Waiting for Security Approval
☒	Inventory Reports.xls	No	Waiting for Construction Approval
🗋	Merger letter.docx	No	Waiting for Construction Approval

- A custom "Procedure Settings" list that contains info about the different teams that should approve the documents in the "Procedures" library. Each item has the team name in the title.

  The list also has a Person or Group column that contains the approvers. For easy testing of the workflow, add yourself as the approver for all teams and change the names when the workflow is finished. This change of approver does not affect the workflow function, so it can be done anytime.

Procedure Settings

Title ∨	Approver ∨
Construction	Peter Kalmström
Legal	Peter Kalmström
Security	Peter Kalmström

25.2 THEORY: COPY AND PASTE

This workflow uses several stages with similar actions and conditions, and to make it easier to create, we use copy and paste. If you copy and paste the original stage/step, you only need to make the necessary changes in each of the pasted stages/steps to make them work as you wish.

Select and right-click on the colored top banner of a stage or step to copy it. Everything inside the stage/step will be affected, so be careful when you make your selection. If you, for example, want to remove a step inside a stage or step, you must make sure that you have selected only that step and not the superior stage/step.

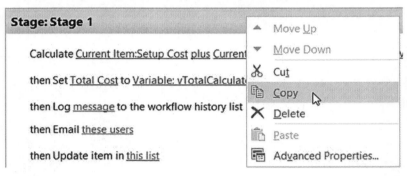

To paste, click on the orange line at the place where you want to paste. It happens that content is lost when you copy and paste workflow parts, so check that everything looks correct.

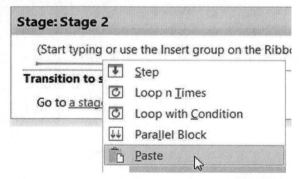

When you paste a stage, you will get a warning that the stage already exists. Click OK, and the new stage will automatically get the name 'Stage [NUMBER]' which you then can change to a more suitable name.

Actions and conditions can also be copied and deleted by right-clicking. In the example workflow Merge Orders in a Tasks List in chapter 28, we take advantage of that to create multiple workflows with a copied action that is adapted to each workflow.

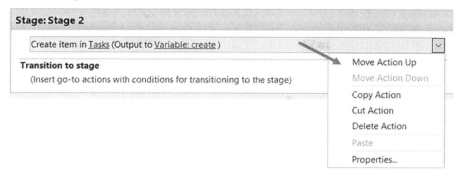

25.3 STEPS

Each approver in the process is represented by two stages in this workflow: one stage for task creation and approval and one stage for rejection. The workflow can be used for any number of approvers, as long as they are more than one. Just create as many stages as you need!

We first create all the more elaborate stages. Each of these stages include a task creation action for a specific approver and a condition that specifies what will happen if the new procedure is approved.

After that, we create the stages for rejection. They are easier, because if one approver rejects the new procedure the workflow will go to the end. These stages are needed to update the *Procedures* list with information about which team rejected the new procedure.

When we create the workflow this way, we can test the task creation and the status update of the *Procedures* list for approvals first and correct any mistakes before we add the rejection stages.

1. Create a list workflow for the *Procedures* library.

2. Rename the first stage to "Waiting for Construction Approval".

3. Add the Action 'Assign a Task', (which you can find under 'Task Actions' in the Action dropdown) for the Construction team approver:

   a. Click on 'this user'.

   b. Click on the ellipsis at 'Participant'.

   c. Select 'Workflow lookup for a User...'

   d. Click on 'Add'.

   e. In the 'Lookup for Person or Group' dialog, select the "Procedure Settings" list >Approver >Email Address. Then select 'Title' and write in "Construction".

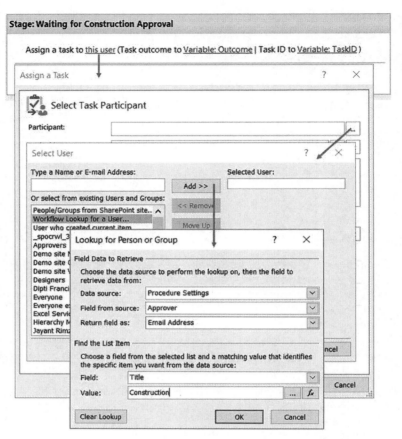

f. When you click OK to the dialogs, you might get a warning that the workflow will not guarantee the return of a single value. This can be ignored, so click 'Yes' to continue.

g. For the Task Title, open the String Builder, add some hard-coded text and a lookup for the Name of the Current Item.

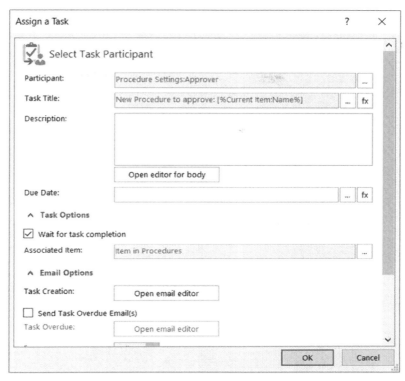

h. I recommend that you use all the default settings, but it is especially important that you make sure that the box 'Wait for task completion' is checked. The approvals should come in sequence, not in parallel in this workflow.

i. Let the rest of the action string be as it is.

4. Add the condition 'If any value equals value', to check if the new document was approved by the Construction team or not:

a. Click on the first <u>value</u> and then on the Function Builder icon.

b. Select 'Workflow Variables and Parameters' >'Variable: Outcome'.

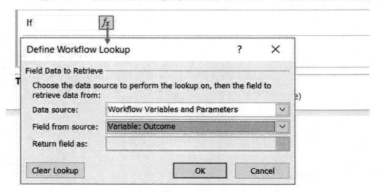

Stage: Waiting for Construction Approval

Assign a task to Procedure Settings:Approver (Task outcome to Variable: Outcome

If [fx]

Define Workflow Lookup   ?   ✕

Field Data to Retrieve

Choose the data source to perform the lookup on, then the field to retrieve data from:

Data source: Workflow Variables and Parameters   ▽

Field from source: Variable: Outcome   ▽

Return field as:

Clear Lookup   OK   Cancel

c. Click on the second <u>value</u> and select 'Approved' from the dropdown.

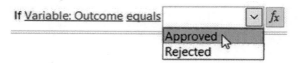

If Variable: Outcome equals [▽] fx
    Approved
    Rejected

5. Add the action 'Update List Item':

   a. Click on 'this list'.

   b. Keep the Current Item and click on 'Add'.

   c. Set the field 'Construction Approved' to 'Yes'.

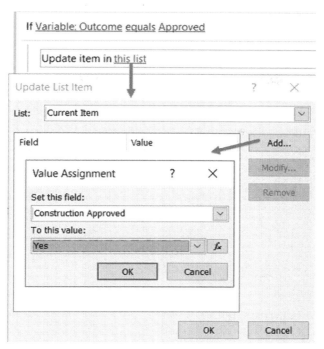

d. Click on 'Add' again and set the field 'Construction Approved By' to the value of the Construction Approver from the "Procedure Settings" list: Open the Function Builder and select the "Procedure Settings" list >Approver >User Id Number. Then select 'Title' and write in "Construction". (This is the same as in 3e above.)

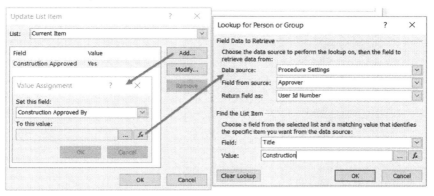

6. Copy the whole "Waiting for Construction Approval" stage and paste it below that stage.

7. Rename the stage into "Waiting for Security Approval".

8. Modify the new stage so that it points to the Security team:

a. Set the 'Assigned To' in the task to the Security team by changing the written 'Title' value from "Construction" to "Security".

b. In the 'Update List Item' action, replace 'Construction Approved' with 'Security Approved' and 'Construction Approved By' with 'Security Approved By'. In the "approved by" Lookup, change the written 'Title' value from "Construction" to "Security".

9. Copy the Condition under the Task assigning action in the "Waiting for Construction Approval" stage and paste it in the Transition step of the same stage.

10. Write "go to" in the 'If' script of the "Waiting for Construction Approval" stage Transition step and press Enter. Click on 'a stage'. Select the stage "Waiting for Security Approval" from the dropdown.

11. At 'Else' write "go to" under and press Enter. Click on 'a stage'. Select 'End of Workflow' from the dropdown.

Stage: Waiting for Construction Approval

Assign a task to Procedure Settings:Approver (Task outcome to Variable: Outcome | Task ID to Variable: TaskID)

If Variable: Outcome equals Approved

    Update item in Current Item

Transition to stage

If Variable: Outcome equals Approved

    Go to Waiting for Security Approval

Else

    Go to End of Workflow

Stage: Waiting for Security Approval

---

12. Copy the whole "Waiting for Construction Approval" stage again and paste it under the "Waiting for Security Approval" stage, so that you get a third stage for the Legal team.

13. Rename the stage into "Waiting for Legal Approval" and make the necessary changes:

a. Set the 'Assigned To' in the task to the Legal team by changing the written 'Title' value from "Construction" to "Legal".

b. In the 'Update List Item' action, replace 'Construction Approved' with 'Legal Approved' and 'Construction Approved By' with 'Legal Approved By'. In the "approved by" Lookup, change the written 'Title' value from "Construction" to "Legal".

14. Copy the Condition from the "Waiting for Construction Approval" stage again and paste it in the Transition step of the Security stage.

15. Write "go to" in the 'If' script of the Security stage transition step and press Enter. Click on 'a stage'. Select the stage "Waiting for Legal Approval" from the dropdown.

16. At 'Else' write "go to" under and press Enter. Click on 'a stage'. Select 'End of Workflow' from the dropdown.

17. Add a new stage to update the "All Approved" column. Call the new stage "All Approved".

18. Add the action 'Update List Item':

   a.   Click on 'this list'.

   b.   Keep the Current Item and click on 'Add'.

   c.   Set the field 'All Approved' to 'Yes'.

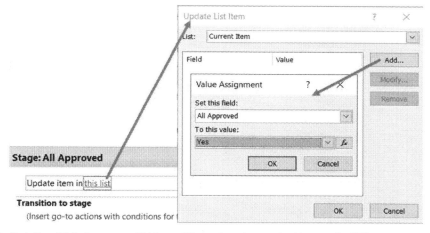

19. Set the "All Approved" Transition step to go to the end of the workflow.

20. In the Legal stage, write "go to" under the Transition condition 'If' script and press Enter. Click on 'a stage'. Select the "All Approved" stage from the dropdown. At 'Else' write "go to" under and press Enter. Click on 'a stage'. Select 'End of Workflow' from the dropdown.

21. Check, publish and test the workflow. Be sure to approve in all three teams, because we have not yet added the rejection component.

22. Add stages for rejection after each of the existing stages:

   a.   Add a new stage under the Construction stage. This will be the "Rejected by Construction" stage.

   b.   In the Transition step of the "Rejected by Construction" stage, go to the end of the workflow.

   c. Copy the whole "Rejected by Construction" stage and paste it under the Security stage. This will be the "Rejected by Security" stage.

   d. In the stage "Waiting for Construction Approval", change the Else condition to go to the "Rejected by Security" stage instead of going to the end of the workflow.

   e. Copy the whole "Rejected by Construction" stage and paste it under the Legal stage. This will be the "Rejected by Legal" stage.

   f. In the "Waiting for Security Approval" stage, change the Else condition to go to the "Rejected by Legal" stage instead of going to the end of the workflow.

23. Set the workflow to start automatically when an item is created.

24. Check, publish and test the workflow.

Demo:

https://www.kalmstrom.com/Tips/SharePoint-Workflows/Approvals-Multiple-Tasks.htm

26 SET TASK ASSIGNEE DEPENDING ON CATEGORY

When people fill out an order or a support or issue tracking ticket in a SharePoint list or form, they seldom know the name of the person who will take care of their request. That value must be set manually – or by a flow.

What people know, or can figure out, is what category their order or issue belongs to, and from that information we can let a workflow pick the default responsible for each item from a settings list. The default responsible can either manage the request (which should be happening most often) or assign the ticket to someone else.

If a person needs to be replaced as default assignee, just edit the settings list and set a new default assignee. The workflow will not be affected. It will continue to run as before and just show the new person as responsible for that category in the tickets.

26.1 PREREQUISITES:

- A *Tickets* list built on the Tasks template with a custom Choice column for "Ticket Category". This column is mandatory to fill out.

  The 'Assigned To', column has a description that tells that it will be filled out by a workflow. Multiple selections are not allowed in 'Assigned To'.

  Users fill out the *Tickets* list, or a custom form connected to that list, with a task name and a description and select ticket category from a dropdown.

- A custom *TicketRules* list where the 'Title' column name has been changed into "Comment". This column does not require a value.

  The *Ticket Rules* list also has these columns:

  o A Choice column for "TicketCategory".

  o A Person or Group column, "DefaultAssignee".

Both lists should have the same choice options in the "Ticket Category" column, so it is best to create a site column that you can re-use, but two list columns will also work.

The flow will work even if you don't enter a default assignee for all ticket categories.

26.2 THEORY: RETRIEVE A VALUE FROM ANOTHER LIST

This workflow can be difficult to understand, so I have used CamelCase naming in the visible names in the *TicketRules* list and columns to separate the lists further.

We use the action 'Update List Item' for the "Assigned To" field in the *Tickets* list item that triggered the workflow. The tricky part is of course to tell the workflow to fetch the default assignee from the *TicketRules* list, and we do that by:

1. Retrieving the value from the "DefaultAssignee" column in the *TicketRules* list as 'User Id Number', which is needed to set a Person or Group type column.

2. Finding the field in the current item that should be filled out with the retrieved value.

The result looks simple, but there are a few steps with Function Builder guides to achieve it.

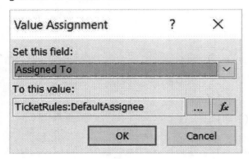

26.3 STEPS

This example workflow runs when a new task has been created in the *Tickets* list. It reads the value of the "Ticket Category" column in the new item and picks the default assignee for that category from a settings list.

1. Create a list workflow for the *Tickets* list.

2. Go to the end of the workflow.

3. Add the action 'Update List Item':

   a. Click on 'this list'.

   b. Keep the default 'Current Item' and click on 'Add'.

   c. In the 'Value Assignment' dialog, select 'Assigned To'.

   d. Click on the Function Builder icon to set the value.

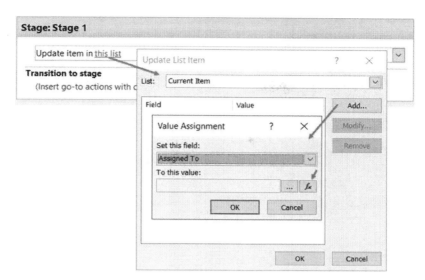

e. Select the *TicketRules* list as Data source and select the Field 'DefaultAssignee'. Return the field as 'User Id Number'.

f. Find the List Item Field 'Ticket Category' in the *Tickets* list.

g. Click on the Function Builder icon at the <u>value</u> field.

h. In the Choice lookup, select the 'Ticket Category' in the 'Current Item'.

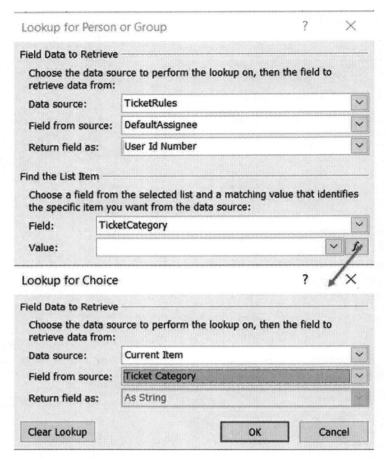

Lookup for Person or Group

Field Data to Retrieve

Choose the data source to perform the lookup on, then the field to retrieve data from:

Data source:	TicketRules
Field from source:	DefaultAssignee
Return field as:	User Id Number

Find the List Item

Choose a field from the selected list and a matching value that identifies the specific item you want from the data source:

Field:	TicketCategory
Value:	

Lookup for Choice

Field Data to Retrieve

Choose the data source to perform the lookup on, then the field to retrieve data from:

Data source:	Current Item
Field from source:	Ticket Category
Return field as:	As String

Clear Lookup   OK   Cancel

4. When you click OK to the dialogs, you might get a warning that the workflow will not guarantee the return of a single value. This can be ignored, so click 'Yes' to continue.

5. Set the workflow to start automatically when an item is created.

6. Check, publish and test the workflow.

27 NEW EMPLOYEE TASKS

When new people join an organization, there are certain things that always must be done. The new employees will for example need some equipment, and the people responsible for arranging that must be informed.

In this example, we will build two different workflows that create SharePoint tasks with information about new staff and what equipment is needed.

27.1 NEW EMPLOYEE TASKS WITHOUT A SETTINGS LIST

In this workflow, each piece of equipment is written into the workflow. This means that the workflow must be changed every time there is a change in the equipment. If you don't do that, the workflow will stop working. Also *refer to* 8.4, Hard-coded Text.

27.1.1 Prerequisites

For this example flow, we need a SharePoint *Employees* list with staff information. New people are added as new items in the list when they are hired.

The list contains three columns: "First name", "Last name" and a choice column, "Position". The choices are "Finance", "Management" and "Production".

The equipment depends on which position the new employee is placed in.

- Finance: a computer and a desk

- Management: a computer, a credit card and an office

- Production: a tablet and protection gear

27.1.2 Theory: Workflow Tasks

In this workflow we use the action 'Assign a Task'. This action creates a task, assigns it to a single Person or Group and tracks its progress.

Assign a task to this user (Task outcome to Variable: Outcome1 | Task ID to Variable: TaskID1)

When creating this action, you must click on 'this user' and enter the task assignee. The two variables can either be kept as they are or replaced by custom variables.

The 'Assign a Task' dialog in *SharePoint Designer* gives several options on what to do with the task. The image below shows the default settings.

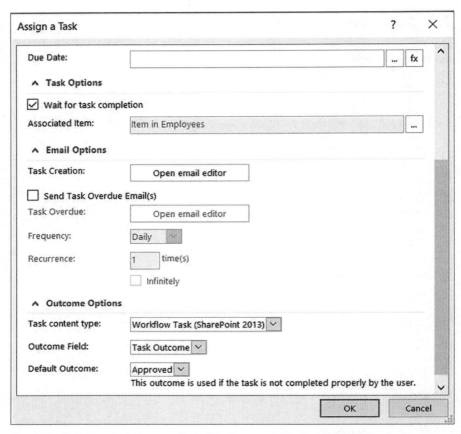

By default, the workflow waits with the next task until the earlier workflow task is completed, but if you uncheck 'Wait for task completion', all tasks will be created at once.

(There is also a 'Start a task process' action, which is used to assign a task to multiple participants, in series or parallel.)

27.1.3 The "Workflow Tasks" List

The first time you publish a workflow to a SharePoint site, a "Workflow Tasks" list is created automatically. All workflows that have tasks, by default use the site's "Workflow Tasks" list, so if you don't change that, all tasks in workflows on that site will be added to the same Tasks list.

We have already seen that the built-in workflows use tasks, and such workflow tasks can also be created in *SharePoint Designer*, under Actions >Task Actions.

Task Actions

Assign a task

Start a task process

The "Workflow Tasks" list is by default displayed in the Site Contents. It is also embedded in the "Workflow Status" page, *refer to* 2.4.1, The "Workflow Status" page.

27.1.3.1   Add "Workflow Tasks" to the Quick Launch

If you add a link to the "Workflow Tasks" list in *SharePoint Designer*, the link will be added to the Quick Launch panes in the whole site.

Go into Lists and Libraries and open the list. Under General Settings you can check the box for displaying the list in the Quick Launch.

General Settings

☐ Display this list on the Quick Launch

☐ Hide from browser

27.1.3.2   Hide "Workflow Tasks"

It is possible to hide the "Workflow Tasks" list from the browser, if you don't use it: open the site in *SharePoint Designer*, go into Lists and Libraries and open the list. Under General Settings you can check the box for hiding the list.

The "Workflow Tasks" list will still be visible if you click on the Preview in browser button in *SharePoint Designer*, and anybody who has the list URL can reach the list, but list will not show up in the Site Contents.

27.1.3.3   Switch Tasks List

Even if "Workflow Tasks" is the default tasks list, you can let some workflows use another list. Any list that uses the Task content type can be used as a tasks list for a workflow. The setting is done in the Workflow settings.

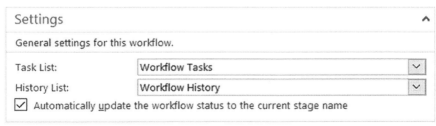

163

Demo:

https://www.kalmstrom.com/Tips/SharePoint-Workflows/Tasks-List.htm
(the first demo)

27.2 STEPS

This workflow first checks if the "Position" value is 'Management. If it is true, the workflow assigns a task for the computer item. Then the workflow creates one task per equipment item. That way it is easy to give different people or groups the responsibility for each item needed by the new employee.

If the value is 'Finance', the process with task creation is repeated but with the items needed for that position, and finally the same process is repeated for the 'Production' position.

In this workflow we will copy and paste actions, *refer to* 25.2, Theory: Copy and Paste.

1. Create a list workflow for the *Employees* list.

2. Go to the end of the workflow.

3. Add the Condition 'If any value equals value':

    a. Set the first <u>value</u> to the current item 'Position'.

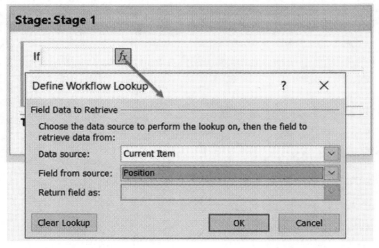

    b. Keep 'equals' and select 'Management' from the dropdown at the second <u>value</u>.

4. Add the action 'Assign a Task' for the computer item.

164

a. Click on 'this user' and select the person who is responsible for the computers.

b. In the Task Title, enter "Computer for" + lookups for 'First Name' and 'Last Name'.

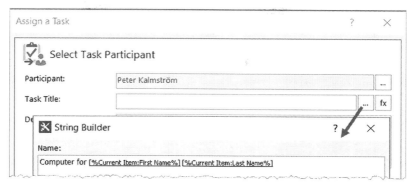

c. Under Task Options, uncheck the box 'Wait for task completion'.

5. Copy the action 'Assign a Task' and paste the copy under the first action.

6. Copy the whole condition with its two actions and paste it under the first condition.

7. Repeat the copy and paste process, so that you have three conditions with two actions in each condition.

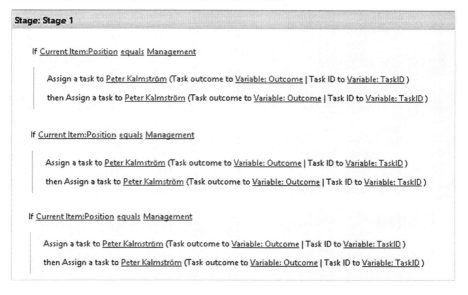

8. Click on 'Management' in the second condition and change the position to 'Finance'. In the third condition, change the position to 'Production'.

9. Click on the assignee name in the second and third condition ('Peter Kalmström' in the image above) and change the parameters so that they fit the Finance and Production positions. *Refer to* Prerequisites above.

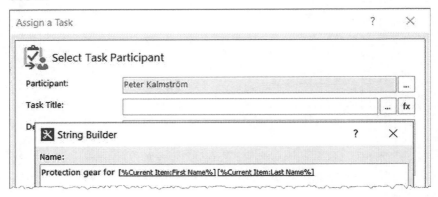

10. In the first condition, copy the action once more and paste it so that you have three 'Assign a Task' actions for the 'Management' position.

11. Change the pieces of equipment in all actions so that you have tasks for all equipment items.

12. Set the workflow to start automatically when an item is created.

13. Check, publish and test the workflow.

27.3   NEW EMPLOYEE TASKS WITH A SETTINGS LIST

To further automate and enhance the process, I recommend that you let the workflow fetch the equipment items from a *Hiring Settings* list instead of hard-coding them. With such a list, you avoid changes in the workflow each time anything including equipment is changed. Even if column values are changed, the workflow will continue to work as before.

When you use a settings list, the workflow may be more complicated to understand, but it is quicker to create. As users can make value changes in the *Hiring Settings* list without disturbing the workflow, this example is much more convenient to use in the long run.

27.3.1 Prerequisites

For this workflow, we need the same two SharePoint lists as in the previous workflow, the *Employees* list and the automatically created

Workflow Tasks list. We are also using the same pieces of equipment for each position as in the previous workflow.

New for this workflow is that we also use a custom *Hiring Settings* list with information about what equipment is needed and which group is responsible for which equipment.

The 'Title' column is renamed to "Position". (In the workflow dynamic content, this column will still be shown as 'Title'.)

The *Hiring Settings* list also has two multiple lines of text columns: "IT To Do" and "Backoffice To Do". These two columns hold the equipment, divided into the two responsible groups. You can use HTML in the description of each piece of equipment.

Position ∨	IT To Do ∨	Backoffice To Do ∨
Managment	Computer	• Corporate Visa • Assign private office
Finance	Computer	Desk
Production	Tablet	Protective gear

27.3.2 Theory: Variable Warning

This example workflow uses two variables, so *refer to* 19.2, Theory: Local Variable, if you need an update on how to create them and set their values.

When you create the variables in this example workflow, you will probably have a warning message that a single value is not guaranteed. This is no problem here, because we only have one value in the Position column.

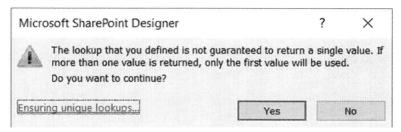

I recommend that you set yourself as responsible first, instead of the IT or Backoffice group that actually has the responsibility for the various equipment items. That way, you can test the workflow more easily.

27.3.3 Steps

For this workflow we first create two local variables for the two responsible groups. These variables read from the settings list which pieces of equipment belong to which group, and they are used in the tasks that are created by the workflow each time a new item is added in the *Employees* list.

1. Create a list workflow for the *Employees* list.

2. Go to the end of the workflow.

3. Create a Local Variable called "ITToDo".

4. Add a 'Set Workflow Variable' action and set the new variable's value to the proper "To Do" value from the *Hiring Settings* list, where the Position of the new employee equals the Position value in the *Hiring Settings* list.

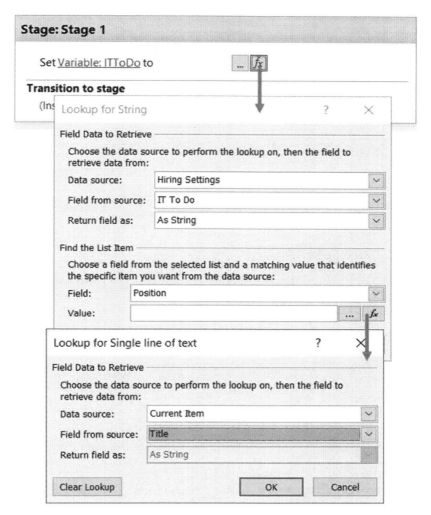

5. Create another Local Variable called "BackofficeToDo".

6. Copy the 'Set Workflow Variable' action and paste the new variable below the first one.

7. Click on 'Variable ITToDo' and change it into the "BackofficeToDo" variable.

8. Click on 'Hiring Settings: IT To Do' and set the 'Field from source' to 'Backoffice To Do'.

Stage: Stage 1

Set <u>Variable: ITToDo</u> to <u>Hiring Settings:IT To Do</u>

then Set <u>Variable: BackofficeToDo</u> to <u>Hiring Settings:Backoffice To Do</u>

9. Add the action 'Assign a Task' for the IT group.

   a. Click on 'this user' and select yourself, for testing, or the IT group.

   b. In the Task Title, enter "New employee:" + lookups for 'First Name' and 'Last Name'.

   c. In the Description field, add the text "These are the tasks:".

   d. Click on the body editor button below the Description field.

   > Open editor for body

   e. Add a lookup for the "ITToDo' variable after the description text.

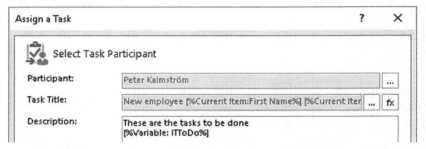

   f. Under Task Options, uncheck the box 'Wait for task completion'.

10. Copy the 'Assign a Task' action and paste it below the first one.

11. Click on the responsible name and replace the "ITToDo' variable with the 'BackofficeToDo' variable in the 'Assign a Task' description.

12. Set the workflow to start automatically when an item is created.

13. Check, publish and test the workflow.

Demo:

https://www.kalmstrom.com/Tips/SharePoint-Workflows/Tasks-List.htm (the second demo)

28 CONTRACTS RENEWAL REMINDER

All organizations have contracts, agreements and subscriptions of different kinds that need to be renewed, and it is a good idea to store such contracts in a SharePoint library. If you do that, you can set a workflow to send a reminder to the person who is responsible for either renewing or cancelling each contract when it expires. Similar reminder workflows can of course also be used for other purposes.

If you have thousands of contracts I recommend that you put them in multiple libraries, with one workflow for each library. To have one library and run this workflow on so many contracts might cause problems.

In this chapter, we will create two reminder workflows:

- A SharePoint 2013 list workflow where we will set the reminder date to seven days before the contract's expiry date.

- A SharePoint 2010 reusable workflow where we first set the date for the renewal to two months before the expiry date.

This example uses a *Contracts* library and a SharePoint 2013 list workflow. Seven days before the expiry date of each contract, the workflow generates an e-mail reminder to the responsible person that the contract is about to expire and must be renewed or cancelled.

28.1.1 Prerequisites

A *Contracts* library with a Person or Group column called "Responsible Counsel" and a Date and Time column called "Renewal or Expiry Date".

28.1.2 Theory: Date Actions

In this example workflow we will use two actions that we have not used earlier in this book: 'Add Time to Date' and 'Pause until Date'. Both these actions are found in the 'Core Actions' group.

28.1.2.1 Add Time to Date

'Add Time to Date' adds a specific time in minutes, hours, days, or months to a date and stores the output value as a variable. Negative time can be used, and in this example '-7' is used to filter out the contracts that expire 7 days after today.

28.1.2.2 Delay Actions

There are some workflow actions that delay the triggered workflow so that it does not run until something more than the trigger has happened:

- The List actions 'Wait for Event in List Item' and 'Wait for Field Change in Current Item' makes the workflow wait for an event or for a specified field to be changed to a specified value before the workflow continues to the next action.

List Actions

Wait for Event in List Item

Wait for Field Change in Current Item

The workflow is triggered when an item is created, but then it runs in pause mode until the specified event or field value change.

It is possible that the specified value is entered already when an item is created, and that is why we use the Created trigger and not the Change trigger. After that, the Wait action waits for subsequent changes in the specified column.

- The 'Pause for Duration' action makes the workflow wait for a specified number of days, hours and/or minutes before it runs.

Core Actions

Pause for Duration

Pause until Date

- 'Pause until Date' sets a workflow to not run until a specified date and time. This means that you can set the workflow to start when an item is created or changed and then use this action to make the workflow wait until a specific date for each item. In this example workflow we set that date to 7 days before the contract should be renewed.

28.1.3 Steps

In this workflow an 'Add Time to Date' action sets the date for the reminder e-mail to be sent and outputs this date to a local variable. Then a 'Pause until Date' action stops the workflow from running until the same date.

Finally, a 'Send an Email' action sends an e-mail to the responsible person on the reminder date, when the workflow runs. All document libraries are built on top of the content type 'Document', which has a Name property used for storing the name of the file. This property is used in the e-mail part of the workflow at point 6c.

1. Create a list workflow for the *Contracts* library.

2. Go to the end of the workflow.

3. Create a Local Variable of the type 'Date/Time' called "ReminderDate".

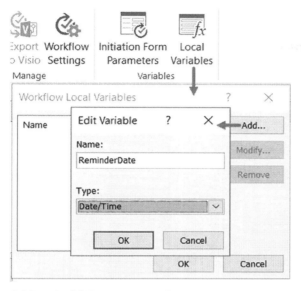

4. Add an 'Add Time to Date' action:

   a. Click on <u>0</u> before 'days' and change 0 to '-7'.

   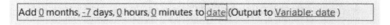

   Add <u>0</u> months, <u>-7</u> days, <u>0</u> hours, <u>0</u> minutes to <u>date</u> (Output to <u>Variable: date</u>)

   b. Click on '<u>date</u>' and set the date to the current item's "Renewal or Expiry Date".

   c. Output the value to the variable "ReminderDate".

5. Add a 'Pause until Date' action and click on <u>this time</u>. Open the Function Builder and select 'Workflow Variables and Parameters' >'Variable:ReminderDate'.

6. Add a 'Send an Email' action:

   a. Click on '<u>this user</u>' and add a workflow lookup for a user.

   b. Keep 'Current Item' and select 'Responsible Counsel' and 'Email Address'.

   c. Open the Subject line String Builder and type hard-coded text: Contract to review. Add a lookup for the Name of the current item.

   d. Add a link to the current item in the e-mail body:

      i. Click on the hyperlink icon.

      ii. Add anchor text.

iii.   At Address, open the Function Builder.

iv.   Select 'Workflow Context' >'Current Item URL'.

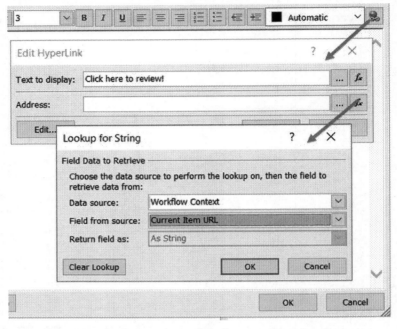

7. Set the workflow to start automatically when an item is created.

8. Check, publish and test the workflow.

Demo:

https://www.kalmstrom.com/Tips/SharePoint-Workflows/WF-Contract-Reminder.htm

29 MERGE ORDERS IN A TASKS LIST

Most companies have a department that handles a lot of different task for the rest of the organization. Here we are using this common use case to show how you can copy content from one workflow to another.

My imaginary department manages deliveries of computers, flowers and tables. As there are three different forms, it is easy to order. Each order form only contains the columns needed for a special kind of item.

We also imagine that the same people will fulfill all the orders, no matter what has been ordered. These people don't want to check orders in three orders lists.

Instead, the handlers want all data that users enter in the order forms to be transferred to one list. This example shows how the transfer can be performed by three workflows, one for each orders list, that fetch data from the orders lists and create new items in a *Tasks* list.

A SharePoint form is always connected to a list, and in this workflow, we are using the lists behind three SharePoint forms. The lists have the same names as the forms. When someone fills out one of the forms, a new item is created in that list. The column values in those list items will be used in the workflow.

29.1 PREREQUISITES

- A *Tasks* SharePoint list built on the Tasks template.

- Three SharePoint order forms/lists, *Computers*, *Flowers* and *Tables*.

  Computers and *Tables* are used for orders within the company, and the 'Title' columns in those lists are renamed to 'Comment' and are not mandatory.

  The flower orders are mostly intended for customers, and its 'Title' column is renamed 'Phone number'.

175

The lists also have the following columns, all mandatory:

o *Computers*: a Choice column, "Type of Computer" and a Person or Group column, "User".

o *Flowers*: a Choice column, "Type of Bouquet" and a Single line of text column, "Recipient". (A Person or Group column cannot be used for people outside the tenant.)

o *Tables*: a Choice column, "Type of Table", and a Single line of text column, "House", with the description text "Please specify where the table should be placed".

29.2 THEORY: CREATE ITEM IN ANOTHER LIST

In these workflows we will use the action 'Create List Item' for the first time and see how it works when a workflow for one list creates items in another list.

When you click on <u>this list</u>, you will have the possibility to choose among all the lists and libraries in the site of the list you created the workflow for.

When you have chosen the list, the mandatory fields are loaded so that you can select a field and click on 'Modify' to set the value.

You can also click on 'Add' to open the same dialog but without a selected field. Then you will have a choice of all the columns in the list, so that you can set field and value.

You can set multiple fields and values, one after another.

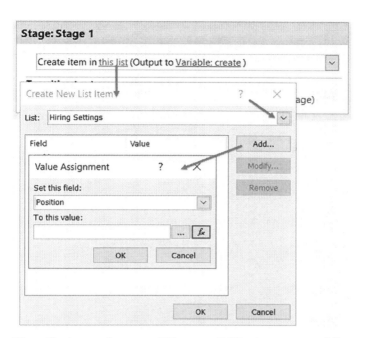

We will also make use of the possibility to copy workflow actions. For this chapter, you might also want to review section 26.2, Theory: Copy and Paste.

29.3 STEPS

These workflows create items in the *Tasks* list, one item for each order. We will start with creating the workflow for the *Computers* list. Then we will create *Flowers* and *Tables* workflows from that.

I recommend that you check, publish and test the *Computers* workflow, after point 5, so that any problems can be corrected before you start copying.

1. Create a 2013 list workflow for the *Computers* list. Call it "New Computer".

2. Go to the end of the workflow.

3. Add the Action 'Create List Item'.

   a. Click on 'this list' and select the *Tasks* list.

   b. Create item in this list (Output to Variable: create)

   c. Among the fields that are loaded, select 'Title' and click on 'Modify'.

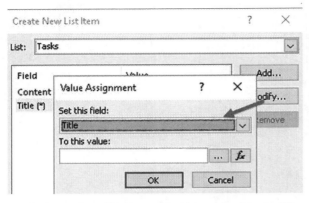

i. Click on the ellipsis at 'To this value' to build a string:

ii. Write "New" and add a lookup for 'Type of Computer'.

iii. Write "for" and add a lookup for 'User'. Return the field as 'Display Name'.

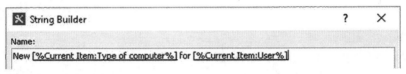

d. Click on 'Add' and select the 'Description' column. As the description has rich text enabled, we can use HTML and add row breaks (<br>).

i. Click on the ellipsis at 'To this value' to build a string:

ii. Write "User" and add two lookups for 'User', one with the return field 'Display Name' and one with the return field 'Email Address'.

iii. Write "Type of computer" and add a lookup for 'Type of Computer'.

iv. Write "Comment" and add a lookup for 'Comment'.

4. Set the workflow to start automatically when an item is created.

5. Check, publish and test the workflow. Keep the tab open, as we need it for the next workflow.

6. Create a 2013 list workflow for the *Flowers* list. Call it "Flowers".

7. Go to the end of the workflow.

8. Open the tab for the "New Computer" workflow and copy the action.

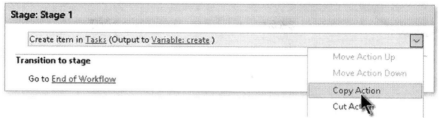

9. Open the "Flowers" tab and paste the action.

10. Click on Tasks and modify the title and description so that they contain dynamic content from the *Flowers* list instead of the *Computers* list.

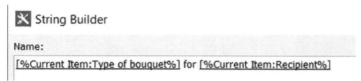

11. Create a 2013 list workflow for the *Tables* list, copy the action from the *Computers* workflow again and change the parameters.

12. Check, publish and test the workflow.

Demo:

https://www.kalmstrom.com/Tips/SharePoint-Workflows/WF-Orders-to-Tasks.htm

30 E-MAIL LINKS

When you create a workflow that sends an e-mail notification when a new item is added to a SharePoint list or library, you probably want to include some links in the e-mail body. Here are some useful links that open documents or items in different ways. Text within brackets in the link code represent dynamic content.

- Library document properties in

  o display mode:
  [Current Site URL][Current List Name]/Forms/Dispform.aspx?ID=[Current Item ID]

  o edit mode:
  [Current Site URL][Current List Name]/Forms/Editform.aspx?ID=[Current Item ID]

- List item properties, displayed in

  o standard mode:
  [Current Site URL]Lists/[Current List Name]/Dispform.aspx?ID=[Current Item ID] OR [Current Item URL]

  o edit mode:
  [Current Site URL]Lists/[Current List Name]/Editform.aspx?ID=[Current Item ID]

- Version history:
  [Current Site URL]_layouts/15/versions.aspx?list=[List ID]&ID=[Item ID] OR &FileName=[Server relative URL]

- Document, displayed in

  o preview mode:
  [Current Site URL][List Name]/Forms/AllItems.aspx?id=[Server relative URL]&ID=[Server relative URL]&parent=[Current Site URL][List Name]

  o edit mode:
  [Current Site URL]_layouts/15/Doc.aspx?sourcedoc=[Server relative URL]

- Alert on item:
  [Current Site URL]_layouts/15/SubNew.aspx?List=[List ID]&ID=[Current Item ID]

- Workflows page for current item:
  [Current Site URL]_layouts/15/workflow.aspx?List=[List ID]&ID=[Current Item ID]

- Current workflow status:
  [Current Site URL]_layouts/15/wrkstat.aspx?List=[List ID]&WorkflowInstanceName=[Instance ID]

- Start SharePoint 2013 workflow:
  [Current Site URL] wfsvc/Copied Workflow Server
  Guid/WFInitForm.aspx? List=[List ID]&ID=[Current Item
  ID]&ItemGuid=[Current Item GUID]&TemplateID=Copied Workflow
  Template ID&WF4=1

Demo:

https://kalmstrom.com/Tips/SharePoint-Workflows/Workflow-E-mail-Links.htm

31 ABOUT THE AUTHOR

Peter Kalmstrom is the CEO and Systems Designer of the Swedish family business Kalmstrom Enterprises AB, well known for the software brand *kalmstrom.com Business Solutions*. Peter has 19 Microsoft certifications, among them several for SharePoint, and he is a certified Microsoft Trainer.

Peter began developing his kalmstrom.com products around the turn of the millennium, but for a period of five years, after he had created *Skype for Outlook*, he also worked as a Skype product manager. In 2010 he left Skype, and since then he has been concentrating on his own company and on lecturing on advanced IT courses.

Peter has published six more books: *SharePoint Online from Scratch*, *SharePoint Online Exercises*, *SharePoint Online Essentials*, *Office 365 from Scratch*, *SharePoint Flows from Scratch* and *Excel 2016 from Scratch*. All are sold worldwide via Amazon.

As a preparation for lectures and books, Peter has created various video demonstrations, which are available on YouTube and at http://www.kalmstrom.com/Tips.

Peter divides his time between Sweden and Spain. He has three children, and apart from his keen interest in development and new technologies, he likes to sing and act. Peter is also a dedicated vegan and animal rights activist.

W

Made in the USA
Middletown, DE
16 August 2019